PRAISE FOR
LIVING WITH THE NEIGHBORS

"*Living with the Neighbors* is a truly beautiful journey of acceptance, healing and empowerment."
- Megan Dunston, MS,
Licensed Clinical Mental Health Counselor

"In *Living With the Neighbors*, Jodi Girouard offers readers an intimate glimpse into her personal world. Such courage is a rarity these days. It is admirable and memorable that she has chosen to speak for people struggling with mental health challenges. Her resilience, strength and vulnerability shine brightly, a model for all who strive to rise above personal challenges.'
- Melissa Lang,
Academic Program Coordinator,
Mercy Connections

"*Living with the Neighbors* is relatable to all women. I am taking my time going through it."
- Dianne Charboneau,
retired teacher and business owner.

LIVING WITH THE NEIGHBORS

ALSO BY
JODI GIROUARD

Body Language; a woman's voice

Faces in the Crowd

"Within the Fields of Possibilities"
an essay included in *Much Madness*

Poetry featured in
Wordgathering, July, 2019

JodiGirouard.com

LIVING WITH THE NEIGHBORS
Poetry and Prose

JODI GIROUARD

DesignWise Studios
Underhill, Vermont USA

Original art by Eleanor Workman

Copyright © 2021 by Jodi Girouard

First Edition, July 2021

ISBN: 978-1098392086

Interior and cover design by Stephen Kastner
Published by DesignWise Studios
DesignWise.net

Manufactured in the United States of America

To my four loving voices,
and to Jocelyn and Jeanie for believing in me

Contents

INTRODUCTION

The Adams Center: A Conversation

Therapist: "Jo, why do you call what you hear the neighbors?"
Jo: "To conjure something less scary than an hallucination. If the noise is just people through the wall talking, then it's not so terrifyingly real."

My Mind's Illness

The silence inside me screams out
a longing to unmask my desperation,
the sadness that surrounds,
the mourning of a normal life.
I practice mindful escape,
dreams of better sounds,
a goodness coaxing me on
instead of the madness.
Music seeps into my senses,
serene sensibilities,
a soothing like being comforted
by a young mother in love.
I listen to the speakers
sending out the voice
of love, of hope, of passion
in this early a.m. of delirium.
I yearn to understand
why I have this disease,
why my insides shout,
why my meaning is questioned.

I put down my thoughts
as the buzzing continues,
the angry mosquito in my ear
with the noise I can't fade from.
A cool breeze from the window
is a breath of reality,
a caress from the outside.
I am okay, I have worth.
I will go lie my head down,
let the swirling conditions settle.
Let my mood evaporate
the harsh insecurities of my illness.
For I am a survivor, floating in the water,
tightening lifejackets on others,
while wrapped in my own.

CHAPTER ONE

The trees in their green coats pressed in as I crouched low into my seat. I traveled between the Green Mountains of Vermont haunted by an unknown scene. A darkness was in my heart, sadness from trauma, despair from the neighbors that haunted me.

I sat beside my sister as the car curled about the river on the winding roads. I watched as we made our way through the valley in Rochester, Vermont, amid the hills. The sun shone down on a normal day for most Vermonters. The light bit into the valley disrupting fragmented shadows, shadows too strong to ignore. Outside, the "neighbors" shouted their curses at me, sneered with derision. I swallowed hard and rolled up my window.

The tires crunched the gravel as the car turned in towards the house. A greenhouse sat beside the farmhouse, plastic that framed seeds just inching out to the sun. I was going to spend time here. This was a peer support home, a place to heal from life's hurts. My sister broke into my thoughts. My young son called to be let out of his seat, and then we were opening the doors to greet the scent of spring.

It was rural Vermont. Fields rolled to the steep mountains just beyond the river on one side. Across the road, trees grew to the edge of a mountain. Green everywhere. Flowers by the road, wild and beautiful in yellows and whites. I didn't smile though. Didn't throw my arms up and embrace the freshness of the day. I took it in, then hung my head with hair covering my eyes.

"C'mon Jo, let's go inside," my sister, Tammy said. She got my little boy out of the car. He reached for my hand

and I took his soft one in my wrinkled one. We walked to the farmhouse with a big white door. A woman opened it and smiled. She wore a flowing sundress that reached down to her sandals, with toes painted pink.

"Hi, I'm Karen. You must be my new arrival." She backed up to let us inside and then closed the door behind her.

I waited until Karen guided us into the room. Her long hair hung loosely down her back. She walked through the kitchen, juggling her weight from side-to-side as she led us into the home. I looked at my surroundings. The farmhouse kitchen featured modern appliances. Beyond the kitchen was a big wooden dining table and beyond that, French doors led to a deck. A sunlit living room was to the right of the dining table. It was open and looked comfortable. A Lhasa Apso wagged its tail.

My little boy grinned and bent to rub her head. The dog licked his lips and I watched as my boy licked back with a chuckle. He patted the dog's head with delight. I tried to smile.

"That's Ladybug," Karen said. "Let me show you your room." She walked through the rooms and down a hall which led to a bathroom and the only two bedrooms. Karen turned left into a room with a double bed. I walked behind her with my sister and son. I put down my bag and looked out the window.

The Green Mountains were on either side of the house. Stillness there. From this room, I could see a line of peaks that stretched beyond the two windows of the room. The pines and tall oaks seemed to crowd in. It was a narrow valley, this town with mountains shooting straight up on either side, a colored wall now holding me in. I took a deep breath and exhaled. This was my resting place for a while, a place to breathe and relax, if I could.

Karen spoke. "Here at Alyssum we are all peer support. The staff have all been through illnesses, been through similar emotions. We are here to help you rest, work through your hardships if you want. We have structured activities like yoga, meditation, gardening. Or you choose how much you want to do. Many people work on arts or crafts that they like. Many walk to the town, or go to the river. You are in charge."

"Mommy, I don't want you to stay without me." My little boy pulled on my hand.

"She won't stay too long," Tammy said.

Tears wet his eyes. Tears wet all our eyes. Karen smiled down at him.

"She's just here for a break. She'll be back home soon," Karen said.

Then she led us back to the living room. Sun lit the room with what should have been refreshing warmth, but I didn't feel it. I felt blackness, an ache inside with much thinking to do. *God, why did I have to do this to my family?*

I scooped my little boy into my arms and squeezed him. My sister rubbed his back. We stood there for a moment, comforting my boy, comforting one another through his small body.

I nodded and then set him down. Tammy took my son's small hand and led him back through the kitchen.

"I'll call you tonight," I muttered as they walked.

"Bye Mommy," my little boy cried out, tears in his lashes.

"I love you guys," I said.

"We love you too," Tammy said. "Try to rest, Jo."

And then they were gone, out the door, into the car, and

down the drive. I watched them go, uncurling their way out of the valley and back home to Chittenden County. I felt sick, didn't know what to do. Karen took control.

"There's lots of things you can do here. Yoga, meditation, peer support with any of the staff. The staff have all been right where you are at one point, they can relate. Here at the retreat center, you have total control to leave, to stay, to share. We're here to help guide you as much as you want."

I let Karen direct me to the table where she took out paper lists and forms to fill out. I spent half an hour letting her talk about the independence I'd have with choices, the beauty of the area.

But all I could think of was the darkness that constantly invaded, seeped into my living, when I just wanted the light. A little more light in my life. That wasn't too much to ask for, was it? And I thought I could reach out and take hold of that light, for I was part of that light.

The Light

Oh, there you are, the light, such a bright friend in
the early morning.
I lift my head to the great warmth,
a date I've missed because of sadness.
I smile into the shine, such a design to overcome depression.
I am alive and fill my need with the will to keep going
on.

For today I am high, flying in the yellow,
trying to capture this sensation,
write it down, forget the times I frowned into the

despair.
It is enough to be here, in this life, this morning,
a wife to my love, a mother to my kids,
a writer soaring on the currents of the sunshine.

The design of my bipolar, a glimpse for others
to see my spectrum, my flow from high to low.
I know it is a disease, it is in my genes
but today is wonderful, my senses not dull
as I cast my eyes to the sky,
to fly in thoughts that are happy, super, wondrous.

Even though I recall the lows, the holes I fall into
I still hold tight to this illusion,
the glorious light that makes my passion lift others,
a gift of words to the world.
God made me this way,
I fall to my knees to pray in the rays
so much like His truth to overcome the gray,
the way my life sometimes is curled beneath my
sheets
with tears, fears, thoughts of death in so many
breaths.

But oh, not now! Today, in the beautiful whiteness,
the happiness that holds my heart,
that wants to share with others this star.
I wrap myself in the beginning of a day
of my journey, to see life in the sensations
I embrace in this morning's sun.

It was such a small thing really. My life was nothing
but a little more light in the world but that was the thing.

A little more of that prism of brightness scattered to others that really did mean something. And I was more than a trifle, more than a pause in the world. I was His gift, and He wanted to share me with the world. If only I would see.

My eyes worked fine; my heart was broken. There was so much pain in the world and so much to lose. I could hear the angry voices, the loud slamming of doors, the turmoil in the very neighborhood I lived in. It pained me to hear them. The screams. The panic. The demands. It wasn't fair.

I knew that didn't matter. There were no assigned lots in life. God wasn't choosing pain for anyone. He was indeed allowing all to muddle through on their own free will. All while having His arms outstretched to all who would choose the light. I wished the small thing was really actually an easy decision to embrace.

I still longed for my weeping willow tree. The place I wrote as a child when all else failed. Hidden beneath the branches draping the ground I used to write there in my backyard. I turned to the room I now stood in. Sunlight still came in, lighting on the couches, on the end tables, the floor where I stood. The voices were loud. I no longer had the tree to hide beneath.

No more branches to slip between, to feel hidden and safe.

The Willow

As a child I slipped between branches of a willow tree
to sit hidden in its shadows draped over me in my
backyard.
I brought a pencil and pad
to trace the outline of a story, the motion of a squirrel
climbing,

the clang of my dad's horseshoes hitting the metal
ringer, or the
whisper of my mom's hands digging in the garden just
up the hill.

I closed my eyes to brush against the long lengths of
leaves, their soft
green touch smooth, clean, a comfort in their being. I
heard my older
brother mowing the side yard, grinding the grass into
the sweet
memory that touched my nose. My sister painted
butter on to burn in
the sun. She flipped a teen magazine, the swish of
each page silky
against her hand, while my younger brother played
matchbox cars
between rows of beans, tracking the cars in the soil
by Mother.

Within the willow's existence
I sat among the roots expelled like arms to hold me,
to cradle
me like my Grandma used to.

With fingers bent around a pencil
I breathed in the normalcy, the okay moments that
didn't come
from a brown bottle reeking of angry words,
distorted thoughts, and dark moments sipped
between bouts of us
being okay.

I wrote a song about the squirrel above me on a
branch,
bees coming out of a hive,
a monarch's splash of color like lipstick painting up
the day. I
licked my lips, hummed a bit, as I wrote it down,
tucked it against
my stomach, and hid it under my bed.

At night I dreamt of middle America where family
debuted wishes
and hopes for each other. I vowed to share my pieces
I collected
beneath the protection of my willow.
Then I had its leaves bent down to circle me like an
embrace,
while I wrote in cover and clung to its branches, even
in sleep.

I wished I had a cigarette to blow out the anger inside.
Anger over my predicament. Ten years almost and I hadn't
touched one, that was indeed something to celebrate. Over
smoke and a smile? No, that wouldn't help, it would hurt
too much.

For I was ten years back again in the same mixed up mess
of emotions that disabled me. What was I doing where I
couldn't think, couldn't move, couldn't feel like my feet
touched the ground?

I missed my husband. I missed his arms around me,
his scent, his breath on my neck. I missed his smile and
his way of wiping away worries. I worried about him and
laughed at the futility of my worry. He was okay, he needed me to be okay.

That was why I was here. I walked about the grounds. I made deep footprints in the farmer's field. I watched young calves chewing on piles of hay as they stared back at me with dark blinking eyes. I sensed there was something here that I was supposed to understand.

Was it the setting upon a path? Was it imprinting onto the world with a movement, a way, a light in the darkness that seemed everywhere?

Was it really such a simple beginning as that? Was it simply a first step, an inspiration, an idea, a moment to shine out and reflect what really mattered in the world? Would that stop the anger, make the neighbors quiet down?

I didn't know. I did know one thing. I knew one small thing really. I did have a light that burned inside... a light inside that I wanted to share with the world. And that mattered a lot and indeed was a simple need, a simple thing really.

Now, I had to figure out the how of it all.

I was there, good or bad; I had made my way to Alyssum, the retreat house, and it felt strange. Silence wrapped around the angry voices and squeezed. It didn't help. I went back to the bedroom that I was going to use.

One of the bedroom windows faced a mountain of trees, pines that reached almost to the sill. Green shades in raised branches, open to the sky. I opened my arms and practiced opening my mind. "Hello God," I said and then sank into the mattress.

Laughter from the other room crushed despair in fragmented happiness. A little reprieve, a little breath, a moment to rethink tragedy. I felt a rush of anxiety about being away and tried to push past it.

Anxiety had other ideas and slammed into my chest, knocked my breath away and made me struggle. I gasped for air, sucked in, and in, and in, and in until it came to me and I could be with my breath. I exhaled and looked back at the view.

The river was out there meandering by the house, flowing on as if nothing ever was wrong in the world. It seemed to call to me, whisper to me quietly, beckon a visit.

I would go and sit by its side. Sit by the rocks and sand and breathe in the solitude of the water. I would grow strong by the careless way the water ran and learn from its mastery of just being. I would be.

I heard the neighbors whispering, threatening with malice. Just the neighbors behind a wall that couldn't hurt, but they did. They broke into my contemplation, eroded my self-will and twisted the truth. I refocused on my breath.

Quieter now. An ache inside for my family. I missed my husband and boys. I missed being able to breathe without pain. Tightness in my arms reminded me of how my husband rubbed my aches away. How the tightness was back but not really in my arms. No, it was in my heart.

I could hear Karen talking to the other guest in the house. They were talking about going for a walk. Part of me wanted to go with them but I still felt so sad about leaving my family that I was rooted to the bed. I closed my eyes and breathed in the moment. One moment at a time and I could get through these moments away. *Just keep breathing*, I thought, again and again in this strange room that I would be staying in for a while.

CHAPTER TWO

I went down to the river. I walked over the farmer's field littered with clay targets between broken cornstalks. Farmer's sons had had shooting practice. I steered away from the manure mound with flies, and walked over the dried, cracked earth to the rocks.

The river rocks shimmered, glared, all meshed together by its side. I was there watching the river twist and turn and race forward. Ever forward, no looking back. It wound its way to me and sprayed about the rocks. It seemed as if it was playing for me.

I watched the rush of water, minnows still, in deep pools, a blanket of soggy sand. I should have brought a shovel. Or my son. Or my love. I thought of them and my mouth opened with an escaped pain. I breathed it back involuntarily. My heart tightened. It tore beneath my chest, ripped, sagged, and then tears trailed down my face. I cried to the river, watched it play, watched life heavy as the rocks I stood by. I wanted to learn to dance like the river. I wanted to live like my children. I wanted to believe.

I was strong, I remembered to come and share, and talk, and learn to deal with my pain.

Strength

Strength found by the leaning tree
Cast over the running, rushing river.
A split decision to hold my own on the bank,
To not fall into the current,
To not dip below the surface of survival,
To find clarity

On the shore of my inspiration.

I sank to the rocks and felt how smooth they had become. Weathered from the water, worn over time, ever time. I wondered if I could still shimmer, dazzle, be bright again and again. This was my time to do things for myself.

I put my hands in the water and felt the cold rush up my arms. The river laughed in a bubbling beautiful way as it traveled over and past me. I felt lighter as my arms waved in the water. It was a start. And the neighbors weren't with me down by the water. It was quiet.

The sun was going down behind the mountain. It cast its shadow on the house as I made my way up the path. Ladybug trotted beside me, stopping to sniff at the grass, and the hay, and the dirt-piled field. She was curious. I remembered being curious about life.

Living in the moment, a person can't help but experience everything before them. I itched to run inside and curl up on the bed but I wasn't ready to go inside yet. The neighbors were starting their tirade and I thought it would be too loud inside.

"You're no good. You should just die. You don't deserve to live."

The neighbors were aggressive. They hurled insults, tried to coax me to choose death. I shook my head. I squeezed my eyes shut in a plea, a prayer, some religious struggle to end this despair. I took in one breath and then another.

I walked Ladybug over to the fire pit and sank down in a chair. She curled up on the side of the chair breathing hard. I looked out at the base of the mountain, the river below, the farmer's field, the green everywhere. I sniffed the air. Pleasant beginnings budded, developed.

Spring was here and with it the possibilities of life. I

looked back at the house. It was a white farmhouse with an attached garage. Flowers were opening just below the windows.

Beyond the house was a gazebo. It was pretty with the setting sun backlighting it. I stood up. Maybe the neighbors wouldn't be so loud. Maybe I wouldn't hear them at all. Or they would decide to go watch TV or sleep, or walk away while I was inside.

I looked back at the piece of property. Mountain tops curved above in the letter C. C for comfort. All about me, spring was lighting the land. Trees grew buds. The grass was greener than before, the land was waking up from its long sleep of winter. I breathed in and it wasn't tight. I breathed out and let any remaining tightness float away. Yes, I was lighter.

I walked toward the house.

"Come on Lady Bug, we're going inside."

The dog trotted beside me as we made our way in.

The night was hard with tears. Wet face, wet pillow, vivid dreams. I tossed back and forth during the night, trying to find comfort in sleep. I woke to the sun and a new chance at breathing. I inhaled the day and rose.

I walked to the kitchen and found some bread to toast. The other house guest was up and walking about the kitchen. Breakfast was organic toast with butter and I tapped my foot as I waited for the toaster to pop. Then, to the table, to bite, chew, swallow. Repeat.

The neighbors were being loud already. It was just before 7 a.m. and they were screaming. There should be a noise ordinance in this town. I bit, chewed, swallowed. Repeated.

The housemate was a young girl and she was cooking eggs on the stove. She leaned against the oven as she waited to flip the soft mess. She was quiet but looked alive with the thought of breakfast. I watched her lift and flip the eggs, grin, then slide them onto a plate.

It was a cheerful morning, no sense of fear. A soft blue sky stretched out before me. I looked around the kitchen and found warmth in the surroundings. It was a homey kitchen with a window over the sink to look out at the front expanse of lawn. Looked like a normal day. I finished my toast and went to shower.

I wondered what my family was doing without me. My husband had called and said, "Your little boy said he missed his peanut butter. I told him that he had it for breakfast. He said, "No Dad, I miss our beautiful girl." I thought that was so sweet.

Today, I would walk to the village with the other house guest. Together, down the road a mile, and then back. I wondered if I was ready. A bluejay rested on a branch by my window. I watched it perch there, vigilant. What did it see that I didn't?

Was it hunting? I wondered. Was it being hunted? I wondered. I thought of the neighbors. They didn't want me around, were so cruel. I tried to race past them to hide but I knew I would have to face them someday. Just maybe not today.

Today was for breathing in the spring. It was for listening to the birds, watching the leaves decide to come out. Yes, it was a day for breathing in hope. It was an Emily Dickinson sort of hope, perched just before me. I reached out towards it, to embrace it. I prayed to be ready.

CHAPTER THREE

I walked out the side door, dragged my feet through the gravel and onto the paved road. I was reluctant to walk to the village but determined not to show it. I walked behind the other housemate.

Silence greeted my slapping feet against the ground and I learned to step lightly. One foot after another, pressing as lightly as I could so as not to disturb.

The river followed us. The river was freckled with those rocks, endless boulders of all sizes and shapes. I walked beside it. The river was quiet here, no murmurs or gurgles or fits of fizzy laughter.

The guard rail seemed to press into me, cars sped by, anxiety walked beside me. I looked at my redheaded housemate and watched as she kept on going. So I too, went on tapping the earth, walking on.

Over a bridge to town, up to quaint houses, looking like such a New England postcard. Houses with porches, spindles, and railings colored brightly against faded wood all in a row in the village. I marched up the hill and looked about.

A used bookstore and bakery caught my eye and I wandered over. I pulled on the wooden door and let the smells of yesterday envelop me. I immersed myself deeply into the possibilities that arranged themselves so neatly on the shelves. I hid in the world of titles that whispered to me in the quiet.

Lost in the moment, exploring with senses, engaged in the act of sensations, I heard the music. It stirred me to walk around. My fingers danced on the spines of the books. Fairies, Hobbits, herbs, and secret gardens sang to me as I lifted the dust from their jackets.

I stopped to crack open a memory of someone I would never know. My hands traveled the page, the smooth paper of another one's story. The smell was comforting, the author, Tennyson. I slid the book back onto its shelf.

The door slammed and the neighbors came in.

"You should die. You are evil. You're no good."

They circled about, laughed at me, told me I didn't belong, didn't deserve to live.

I scanned the self-healing section as they laughed and called me stupid. I tried to hear the music but the men I heard among the neighbors, were too loud.

I left the store, all the used delights and smells, and went to the town square. I chose a bench and looked about. A young toddler with his shoes off was attempting to climb a small hill. *That's how I feel*, I thought.

I watched his toes grabbing onto the earth, pushing him upward. He squealed at the top and raced down as his feet were tickled by the green grass. His laughter met him at the bottom.

Grabbing Earth

Could I relearn to walk his way?
Could I find peace this coming day?
Could I begin to stand then run?
Could I find happiness beneath the sun?
Oh little child of the earth,
I pray you know your worth.
Please show me courage, dear, and true
So I can believe in me like I do for you.

I thought of my youngest son. At a distance the neighbors hooted and laughed at me. I needed to face them but was unsure how to do that. They were so cruel and there was no help to keep them away. People had tried. So many people. But nothing made them stop.

My housemate came and sat beside me on the bench. She said little, just watched the scene at the park. The toddler was trying to climb the hill again, laughing as he fell. I smiled at his ways and turned to my redheaded housemate.

"I'm gonna head back now," I said.

"Me too," she replied.

We continued to sit, quiet beside one another.

"Do you ever wish you could just float away?" I asked. My housemate, my sidekick in depression, the other sad mother with me, kicked her feet out into the air. She looked to the blue field in the sky, swung her legs, looked so far away I thought I would never be able to truly catch her. *Could someone catch me?*

"Sometimes. Sometimes I just want to disappear," she sighed out the last word and hung her head.

"Yeah, I know what you mean."

I stood up and began the walk back with her. Silence between us was comfortable. We walked by the river.

It gurgled a bit in patches of our steps. Large boulders poked their tops out of the cold water. I wanted to jump in and float away. I thought that my housemate seemed to want that too.

I kept walking. Soon my feet and legs were loose, and rubbery. I had my second wind and it felt so good!

I now noticed some pain but didn't judge it, just kept walking.

The wind pressed against my back, cushioning me. I felt alive, outside with the wind and the river. I slapped my foot onto the pavement, pressing myself loudly onto the world.

I am here. I thought. *I am here*.

I slapped my way through the grass by the house, held onto the earth with my own toes, so glad the neighbors were still back in the village.

CHAPTER FOUR

The afternoon passed slowly with stolen moments of writing, talking, engaging in life. I avoided the other patient living with me. I was distracted from the peer support team by the constant noise in my head.

I was asked to go to the river and agreed. There were three of us who walked together through the green patches between the farmer's fields, my housemate and I, as well as a younger peer support person. We watched as a young farmer was out in the hot sun spreading that God-awful manure. We walked on to the path and found ourselves coming up to the top of a small hill. There was the river below us.

The flow curled between banks littered with stones. I walked over them to the edge of the water. I had borrowed knock-off Crocs from another and stood there, gripping my toes on the stones. The plastic shoes molded over the rocks. I didn't stop there but went on, my feet marching me into the water. Soon, I was in up to my calves. My legs sliced through the coldness and my feet formed over the rocks in the cool water below.

The water was so clear, at least there was something today that was clear. My thoughts were muddy, thick as the clay by the far riverside. It was hard to think but it felt good to be outside my thoughts, walking through the river on such a warm spring day.

My housemate was up ahead, her pants rolled way up, her sleeves up over her shoulders. She was almost to the other bank, head down examining the water and its contents. I looked over at the staff member who had brought us down here. She too shared sorrow held back behind her laughter.

The river felt good against my legs. I longed to fall back into it and let it take me. Let it wash me down the bend, floating in clarity as my eyes viewed the baby blue sky. It wasn't that simple, but it could be.

I watched the staff member flick her cigarette over a heart shaped stone, and felt captured in the moment. Moments were so hard to stay within. So much of the past bumped me and jostled me out of the present. So many hurts. Perhaps this was my time now. It was time to relive the bruised, mixed-up mess that still haunted me.

I waded to the shore and sank down onto the dried mud. It pressed beneath me and I settled against driftwood. My body soaked in the sun I craved while my mind traveled back. Way back.

I was thirteen and wanted to be just like my sister. Tammy worked in the mall. I wanted to work in the mall. My sister had a boyfriend at 16, I wanted one too.

My mother had dropped me off at the downtown mall while my sister finished up her shift. Then, we would drive home together. I wandered down to the lower level and into a greeting card store.

There were so many knick-knacks, such perfect replicas of tiny animals, ballet dancers, and fairies. I walked down the aisle of glass shelves, lost in the perfect world of miniatures. The collectibles were in the back, beyond the shelves filled with cards. I didn't realize that I was in the back of the store, and all alone. I kept looking at the small figurines, wishing I had more than just the five dollars in my pocket.

As I turned around, a college man was heading straight for me. I was confused because his pants were unzipped and his penis was standing straight out, coming toward me. He was moving to me, getting closer with his nakedness showing. I was frozen in place.

I looked to my left but there were only more glass shelves with those perfect little figures. I looked to the right and thought I might just squeeze through the gap that separated the next aisle from where I stood.

I didn't wait, I pushed my body through the gap, sucked in my breath, and shoved myself to the next aisle. Fear gripped me. He was still coming towards me and he was laughing. He was touching himself as he grinned at me.

I would never forget that sick smile, almost a sneer. I scraped my stomach against the edge of the shelf but made it to the next aisle. His head poked above the shelves and I could still see parts of him.

I had to get out of there. I ran and he turned and ran towards the front. I turned back and moved next to an elderly lady. The lady smiled and turned back to the greeting cards. I sucked in air, wanted to scream, didn't know how. The lady asked if I was okay. I barely nodded but stayed close to her as we both moved down the aisle.

I looked to the front and saw the man with another friend, jumping up to catch my eye.

They were trying to catch me looking. They were laughing and watching. I couldn't take it, but I dared not move away from this lady. She found a card and made her way to the cashier. I moved behind her and tried to look natural.

I couldn't breathe, couldn't swallow, couldn't wait to find my sister, Tammy. Just get to my sister. At the register, the men were no longer in sight. They were gone. It was over. I was thirteen and I could breathe again.

Tears coursed my cheeks, anxiety stung my insides. I

made my way to the candy store where my sister worked. Sweet Dreams. I fell behind the rows of chocolate and held onto Tammy. I didn't talk then. Later, just not then.

On the riverbank, I stretched my neck. I recalled that past girl but she didn't seem like me anymore. I was older, would have screamed now. Maybe kicked at them, done something. I didn't have to live that pain anymore. I threw the image into the water with a rock. And another rock.

By the Shore

Outside, I find the breath to fling, to bring
my pain into an arced flight to the water's edge.
No longer balanced on a ledge, I was there
by the shore, dredging the shallows for more
stones to seize, to freeze the pain and thrust
from my being, freeing myself from the past.
At last I knelt there below the mountains,
hidden behind plant stalks, and farmer's fields
in the beginning of a possibility of living.

More images swam before my eyes and I let them pass. It was time to unwind all the pain, cast it out to the waters here, in the safety of this retreat. My housemate was still in the water. The staff member sat and smoked by the edge of the water.

God, I almost had one. A long overdue cigarette. Almost. But, I abstained.

I lifted my face to the sun, so warm it broke my heart. I wished my family was with me. I wished they were right here at this river, flinging rocks into the water and watching the current pass by.

The water looked so clean. I wished I felt as clean as the water looked. So much baggage hanging on my shoulders. I needed to keep on taking things out, picking them up and then discarding them.

I stood, and walked back to the water. I plunged my feet into the coolness, stepped over the rocks, trudged through the soft muck on the bottom, felt my feet sink and stick, pulled them free. Memories came, and I let them pass. Like an old film strip, I was in charge of turning past each image.

Up ahead in the river, there were three ducks. They dipped their heads in the water, shook their tails, unconcerned that I was there. I let my fingers dip into the water, then shook my fingertips, scattering droplets, and it felt good.

The mountain came sharply down to one side of the river and its shadow was cast over us. The sun was behind it but the sky was still brightly lit. We played in the shadow of the trees, scooping up rocks to take back to the house.

I was a middle-aged woman selecting rocks to paint words upon. They were something tangible to hold, a weight to carry the baggage instead of keeping it in my heart. Smooth, flat, and thin ones found their way into hands and I gladly lugged them back up to the house.
The neighbors were there as I made my way up from the river with the other two.

"You're no good. You are evil. You deserve to die."

They hurled accusations at me, sneered, and laughed. I let them be, didn't look at them or let them see my fear. We walked up the hill to the house. The neighbors laughed, called me stupid.

I shut the door on them, whispered how stupid they were, and went inside.

That night, I painted two rocks. Painted them white with hues of pink and blue. I would paint words on them if I could figure out just what I needed to say. I closed my eyes and thought of all I had left behind.

Untitled

It is enough to simply be myself
in this moment, a canvas for
creating, the baggage beginning
to drop. I am here in this time,
one brush stroke upon another
building a better breath, creating
a beginning to an endless
masterpiece.

I missed my family but now I was here, so I could be more alive and more whole when I returned to them. If that made any sense, I wanted to heal and was sure there was something more than just medicine that could do that.

My hands had white drops of paint on them and it reminded me of the toddlers I cared for, how they loved to squish, and squeeze, and explore paint. I laughed a bit and pushed my thumb and pointer finger together, rolled the paint between, and laughed at my silliness. Laughter was good.

So was painting. I picked up my brush and added another coat onto each rock.

CHAPTER FIVE

In the morning, I went for my second walk to the village. Outside of the house, I found Karen in the greenhouse. Karen was the peer support person for the morning. The staff at the retreat center changed frequently, but I liked Karen. Karen was tending to the small shoots of spring that she was growing.

"Hi there, spring is really here," she said as she kept her eyes on the tiny green plants.

"I'm going for a walk," I said softly.

"Oh, it is a nice time for that. Enjoy it."

I walked out of the warm greenhouse and set foot on the graveled drive. I felt the hardness of the ground as I traced it to the road. Out on the road, my sneakers slapped against the pavement. A rhythm beat into my mind, and I breathed with each slap of my feet.

I focused on my breathing and encouraged myself to go to the next tree or just to the next telephone pole. Just to keep walking and breathing was all I needed to do.

My ankles hurt, my sideache flared up, but I kept to the rhythm. The river lapped along beside me and I welcomed its conversational sounds. I stopped at a culvert and looked across the street.

A waterfall thrashed itself down the mountainside, then right beneath the road, and finally right beneath my feet. It rushed out a culvert and down to the river below. There was so much energy running through it, running beneath my feet.

I wished to tap into it, place my hands flat on the pavement and feel its movement as it raced to the river and onward. I wanted to capture the shower of water that fell, and feed my tiredness. I closed my eyes and focused on my breath, daring to be the water. A moment later, I walked on.

I passed the condemned house with its garage, twenty feet from where it should have stood thanks to Hurricane Irene. I passed the new concrete bridge, and the older temporary bridge along side. Up a small hill, and I was back to the village. I had made it.

There was Sandy's Book and Bakery with the used books. The General Store on the right. Hardware store on the left. I made my way to the town square and sat on a bench to rest my ankles.

An elderly woman sat on another bench, smoking. *Of course she is*, I thought. I wondered if in another twenty years I would be that woman, dragging on a smoke, watching youth rush past.

I turned my attention to the old church turned library. I wanted to go there but it wasn't open until the afternoon. So, I watched the cars, the bikes, and the walkers. Across the way, college-aged kids sat on a porch eating breakfast. A waitress filled their cups with coffee.

I had never liked coffee. Too bitter. I liked Diet Coke.

I rubbed my eyes. Thoughts coming. I was fading back from them. The square grew faint as I gave in to the need for another memory.

I was escaping from the psychiatric floor. A nurse on the ward sat in the office tapping her pen on a clipboard. I was a girl, seventeen then, and I crept below the window so as not to be discovered.

My two cohorts, a bulimic, and another depressed teen, crept along beside me. We made our way down the hall which seemed to grow longer as we tried to reach the door.

It was unlocked and we quickly slipped out and down the hall.

We crouched as we walked to the elevator and waited for the loud ding to let us aboard. Once inside, we all took deep breaths and exhaled nervous energy. We were headed to the ground floor of the old part of the hospital.

The psych ward was patched together between two floors in the old part of the hospital. The old elevator took us right to the ground floor and to the massive wooden door that led outside.

I pushed on the latch and breathed in the cool winter air as I made my way outside. My bare toes curled up as they touched the white carpet of snow, so cold it felt sharp. I let out a high-pitched squeal and jumped from foot to foot through it. Grass and weeds cushioned my walk beneath the layer of snow and it felt comforting. It felt real.

I lifted my hands to the snow falling and watched the flakes wet my skin. It gave a much needed voice to the sky. I didn't want this to end. I spun about in the white spots that lit up the darkness. It was beautiful.

I looked over at my two friends, one was smoking, of course, and one had her face turned to the falling snow. We were all just girls. Just teens. Just messed up.

But out here, there were moments without doctors, moments without therapists in corduroys. Why did every therapist own corduroy? Well, out here there were no more med checks, no more shots, no more blood tests, and no more parents shaking their heads and wondering what they did to deserve such troubled children.

I lifted my hands to the snow again, felt the flakes turn to water dripping down my arms. An alarm sounded. Ah, they discovered we were missing. But we couldn't be seen yet, girls playing in the snow. We had a little more time.

All three of us seemed lost in our own moments. A solitude shared together.

The snowflakes danced down in the light of the street. We turned in our spots, reflecting raw thoughts as the crystals coated us.

The movement spun us in a decision to do nothing but sway and catch the falling ice. To smile with satisfaction in the futile moments before our discovery. We blended with each other's sorrows, captured one another's sentiment placed in swollen hearts overflowing with the ripe pain of the season.

I blinked in the sunshine. No snow here just a warm spring day in an unfamiliar park. No doctors or therapists either, just peers supporting one another amidst the trees of the Green Mountains.

I looked at the elderly woman sitting on the bench before me and hoped to meet my own self in another twenty years. Maybe I'd come here wearing corduroy. I grinned and liked the idea.

CHAPTER SIX

On the way home, I was stopped by a man in a pick-up truck.

"Hey baby, need a ride?" the man grinned at me through the passenger window.

"No thanks, " I said as I kept moving.

The man put the truck in reverse and peered at me through the passenger window again.

"I thought you wanted me to stop."

"No thanks." I was walking in the opposite direction of his truck. Why would he think I wanted him to stop?

"C'mon," he called through the open window. A sick grin on his face. "You know you want a ride."

I kept walking. He followed in reverse. I just kept walking, not looking, not inviting any conversation. Finally he put it in gear and drove off.

For a while, I wondered if it was him as each car and truck passed from behind. I was careful to stay on the side facing oncoming traffic, but it did little to help my anxiety. Each car that passed was a reminder that danger could come from anywhere. Even up here in the middle of the Green Mountains.

I tried to focus on just getting to the next telephone pole, the next twenty steps, the next bend in the road. I could see the house, but it was still a few hundred feet away and I was tired. I hoped Karen was still out by the greenhouse. If I could only get to Karen.

My thoughts gave away my distress, so I tried other thoughts to rid myself of the anxiety. My PTSD was raging inside. Fears from past trauma came at me, pushed their presence into my mind. Scared me.

I thought of my family. I missed them so much.

I wished that I felt better. I wished the neighbors were different. I remembered the first time I had met them. They had always terrified me. I had tried to ignore their existence.

I didn't tell anyone how cruel they were to me. I kept them and their hurtful ways to myself.

I had just turned twenty-five when I first heard them. They screamed at me, tried to get my attention as I worked as a preschool home visitor in the Champlain Islands for Head Start.

"You're no good. You should die."

I was in my car. My office in the remote countryside. Chills on my neck. What was I hearing?

"The world is better without you. Die. Kill yourself. Just die."

They shouted curses, sneered at me. I wouldn't lift my eyes from the steering wheel. I gripped the wheel tight. Tried to breathe. Tried to make sense.

"Hey Stupid! We're coming to get you."

They hurled words at me. I couldn't tell where they came from but I could still hear them.

"We're gonna get you."

I locked the car doors, listened to the neighbors' loudness, and pressed my head between my hands. I squeezed my eyes shut, tried not to listen to what they were saying about me. I was alone with no one to help me find comfort up here in the islands in Vermont. I rocked myself in the driver's seat as I cranked the radio and cried, and cried.

Tossed About

Insults tossed and spread
like dough pounded into my mind,
coating my senses, leaving me sliced up
in the delirium.
My mind's panic
thrusts at the present
with the harsh noise
heating the inside of my car.
I bleed and there is no one
to bandage my
soul.

Now, back as a middle-aged woman, I inhaled and let the air back out. *Just keep breathing*, I thought as I turned down the drive to Alyssum, to the farmhouse.

I spotted Karen by the greenhouse as I walked down the grass towards her. Karen turned and waved. *She doesn't know what happened*, I thought. *If I could just get to Karen everything would be okay.*

I stumbled up the gravel drive to Karen. I was there, I had made it. Karen greeted me and quickly asked if I was okay.

I stayed with Karen, talked it over, found a bit of courage and strength to recognize I had handled things right. I was in control. I stayed with her as we walked to the house.

"I felt totally helpless," I said. "Felt like I couldn't control what was happening."

Karen touched my shoulder. She smiled, her long white hair waving in the gentle breeze. A kind hippy.

"You did control it. You kept on walking. You did it."

"I did it," I repeated. "I took care of myself."

We talked it over and talked it over again. I was no longer that young, thirteen-year old, nor a teenager unable to care for herself. I was strong. This episode had triggered me, set off anxiety's spiral, but I had actually handled it well.

Karen's words validated. I needed to realize I was a grown woman and could, indeed had, taken care of myself.

Later, my mother would call and ask me to no longer walk alone. For tomorrow, I had another companion in my housemate. After that, I would have to see if I needed one. I would consider it.

I thanked Karen and went to hide in my room. No, not to hide. Maybe just to write, yes writing was good.

That night, we ate tuna steaks with crumbled crackers, butter, and lemon juice. It was delicious. I tasted each bite, letting it fill my mouth with its flavor.

I settled into the living room and tried my hand at yoga for eighteen minutes. A record! It really stretched me, and I cracked in many joints. And it felt good.

Later in the evening, I worked on my breath. In and out, a rhythmic balance. I worked at it while listening to Jess, the evening staff member, and my other housemate, laughing at comedy.

I was sore from the day's exercise, both body and mind.

Ladybug came and curled up next to me on the floor. I rubbed the Lhasa Apso. Peace with a friend.

I had been studying contemplation and was practicing just being with God. Distractions surfaced and I tried to push them away. Maybe the yoga breathing would help with it. I closed my journal and lay on the bed.

In and out, in and out. *Peace is flowing*, I thought. *I am here. Fill me up.* I didn't need to know the how, just that He wanted to help. So did I.

Time passed and I rubbed my eyes. Relaxation, meditation, and prayer-life all led to sleep. No nightmares though.

I looked out the bedroom window. Rain cried down the glass in depressing currents. The green view was all wet, so I sank back onto the bed.

A good memory now. Aah, the moment when my little boy met Mickey Mouse this past January. His face shone, his eyes bright, a grin to the mouse. He had hugged Mickey and it had been worth the hours of layover in the airports, the traffic, the money, just to get to this joy. He elevated everyone's life.

That was magic.

CHAPTER SEVEN

My husband wrote to me online and it was so wonderful to read his words. His love came through in encouragement so clear. I still couldn't believe how he loved me, so devoted and so many years together. We had been seventeen when we started dating. We had grown together over the years until we were as one life, each needing the other to keep on. I missed the way he held me, the way we laughed at our youngest son's antics. Our two older boys were grown, adulting. I missed them all. Especially my love.

I sprawled on top of the pink comforter on the bed. It was still raining and blanketed with such thick fog. I looked out into the wetness. My thoughts were not as muddy or dense as the outside. Not fearful.

A bird flew into the soupy fog, disappeared. I thought back to yesterday when I had seen a white and black duck with red beak and red feet. It had been swimming in the river. I had never seen one like it before. He was so different looking, such a different beauty. I watched him swim as I stood by the side of the river.

I wondered what it was like to never notice another life. Never notice someone off to the side, never freeze up, never wait for the pain to come.

I used to know how that felt. And in fact, I would again. That was why I was here at this place. All that wetness outside, eventually the wind and sun would dry it away, clear up the view.

I focused on my breath, drove out intrusive thoughts, cleared a path to travel down, and chose to remember.

On the sill, were the rocks I had picked from the riverside. Some stacked, some painted, some on their own, apart from the other groups. I let my thoughts pass by like the river, an endless stream of memory.

It had been raining then. Raining hard. My wipers were slapping at the downpour, but doing little good.

Around a corner, I spotted the boy. He was soaked and standing with his thumb out. I should have driven past, should not have cared that he looked so cold. I did neither.

Pulling up to the curb, I watched as he opened the passenger door and got in. Rain slid off his cropped Afro and onto his small shoulders.

"Hey thanks, it's wet out there!"

I smiled, a nervous response. Already I was unsure of what I had just done by picking this boy up. He talked about high school, how he went to Burlington, just down the avenue we were heading.

He chatted on, I nodded, feeling myself relax. I wondered how far down he needed to go.

"I'm not going too much farther," I said after a few minutes. "Heading to my boyfriend's house."

"Drop me as far as you're going. It's cool."

Silence then. A mile further, I pulled off the main road and onto my boyfriend's street. I stopped by the curb, waited for the boy to get out.

He didn't.

In fact, he reached out and grabbed onto my right breast. Squeezed it as he pushed his body onto me. Pushed his face onto my face, his lips onto my lips. I couldn't breathe, it hurt. I shoved him off of me.

"C'mon baby." He got back on me and squeezed my breast again. I hit him, pushed him hard. He sat back on the other seat.

I slapped him hard. He tried again to get on top of me. Why didn't I honk the horn? Why didn't I scream?

"Get out!" I hurled the words at him, as I shoved him farther away.

"You wanted this," he said.

I shook my head, tears sliding down my view of the window.

He got out and I locked the doors. I pushed my mini skirt way down to my knees, fluffed my hair, and tried to compose myself through my sobs. I tried to breathe slower, calmer. I was safe now and could go find Jim, my boyfriend, the one I was to marry, who always made sense of things. He would comfort me, hold me and it would be all right again.

I had been trying to help another. I wanted nothing more than to help.

Composed, I let myself into my boyfriend's home. I sank into a chair behind the kitchen door. Jim came to me and I wept in his arms. Oh, how I cried.

I opened my eyes. Yes, a woman now. I was back on the pink comforter in the room in the Green Mountains. I was safe. I let the memory sizzle out in the fog, and evaporate to nothing. I wasn't that helpless girl anymore. Actually, I hadn't been helpless then either. I had made my needs known.

It wasn't until much later that I learned Jim had found out who had attacked me and hurt him back. I didn't want to know what he had done. Justice? I wasn't sure.

I did know one thing. Jim really heard me. I was never invisible with him.

The neighbors were loud, calling to me, yelling my name.

"Jo-di! We're coming to get you. Jo-di!"

My name, they wanted to haunt me, make me hide, shrivel up. I would not.

I would not be another victim. I would face them, talk back to them. Confront their anger.

But not yet. I needed to think how to do it, what I would say. Had I ever liked myself? Yes.

As a child I had really loved myself.

My parents told stories of when I would sit and sing to an audience. How I would light up and sing with such emotion, such a smile as I sat in a high chair. It made them happy. I liked making people happy. Still do. I wrote poetry often for others. I handed them out to uplift others, make them realize they were a gift to the world.

I remembered the hill behind the home I grew up in. And the kids in the neighborhood meeting up there to play.

Pine trees and red rocks to climb. Forts to build, house to play. Safety up there on the hill. I always hated when a friend's mother rang the bell which meant it was supper time and time to end our play. Transitions were always hard, even then.

I could still picture the path up to the hill between the pines seeded in straight rows, then twisting through small trees bare of leaves. Sometimes, I would look in the tree branches at a bird's nest. I searched for the blue eggs of robins and sometimes found them. I was always careful not to touch them for the mother-bird may not like my scent and abandon the nest.

I saw the hill through young eyes once more. The gentle slope through the hillside, walking upon a rabbit's worn trail. And then, I saw rabbits hopping away from my sight. Up to the rocks we used as a fort. Sandstones with the white lichen we played upon. Pricker bushes surrounded it, sharp thorns that cut. From the back of the cluster, was a path that let in to our rocks, our fort.

I would trace the white patterns of lichen on the rocks as I sat there, hidden from sight.

The big rocks made up different rooms that we played in. A kitchen, a bedroom, a living room.

One rock looked like a piano and so many times I had stopped to pretend to play music.

The kids from the neighborhood gathered there and played after school and on vacations. Milkweed pods became food for us to gather and store. Outside of the rock cluster was a rock with a sitting indentation and we would sit there looking out over our land. We would pretend to fish with the long cattails we found. It was a time of simple innocence that I found pleasure in reliving. I would take a journal and write about it.

The Hill

The past was before me, up our hill calling out from
present shadows that draped about me like a shawl
weighing me down.
I wanted to believe in more than just the desperation,
the
belief that life was all mourning. So I walked between
trees,
void of Fall, the ground littered in yellows, reds,
brown.
Felt the clumps thick under clogs that struggled to
stomp
away sadness with each step up my childhood hill.
I wanted to experience the time before, when I was
small

enough to remember
to check nests for forgotten eggs. Where the birch
trees
just ahead were a maze of whiteness that lit the day.
Where I was lost within the branches of a beautiful
story,
no longer misplacing memories.
I traced a finger in an old pile of dirt with weeds like
ivy covering the old debris.
We played here.
I closed my eyes to see my brother, and neighbors
Scott,
and Jimmy now gone.
Jimmy who smiled at me with his eyes, a ten-year old,
enchanted.
He built me forts, he whittled limbs down for me to
climb.
We sat in pine trees, laughing,
creating a world that didn't belong to adults.
I opened my eyes and longed to see him here at our
view.
The end of Autumn was wet and wilted and my feet
were cold.
I stood and huddled in my winter coat, feeling it was
too soon worn. I
walked to the giant boulder where we sat to fish for
milkweed pods, to gut
their seeds open, to let them fly in the wind with our
dreams.
The pods were now cracked, the guts stuck.
I pulled the fluff out and threw it to the sky.
Laughter chased me, an echo from before as I rushed
down the hill,

through the birch trees, the empty trees, the prickers
that bit at me but I
didn't feel. I stopped and looked up at our fort,
thought I could see Jimmy bent over a tree, cap on,
whittling for
another at our secret place. I wanted to remember
him there like
our youth, as I discovered I still liked climbing trees,
liked the soft
ascent with sap on fingers, liked our verses chanted as
we spied
rabbit holes and burrows. As I realized peace and
passion could
still occur
in an afternoon breathing without tears, burning to
learn a child's
way shared, like an empty bird's nest capable of holding the future.

From school, to home, to play, and back. So many
different people to spend time with, to get used to, get ab-
sorbed with, and then to have to say goodbye.

I hated goodbyes. Hated having to end one moment for
another. Life was all transitions and it was hard.

I remembered youth group retreats from church. How
I felt so close to the group, and so sad when it was time to
go home. Away on a weekend retreat I would grow close
to the other kids, listen to speakers talk of overcoming
pain and finding God. It brought me back to the times
when life had seemed perfect, the closeness between people
shared. It brought me back to childhood on the hill.

I recalled being fourteen and coming home one day in

June from such a beautiful weekend. My parents had been busy, so a friend's mother had brought me home. I felt alive and wanted to share this joy.

I couldn't wait to share it with my family. It was quiet at the house. Only my dad's car was in the drive. Usually my mom's, my sister's, and my older brother's cars were arranged in the large drive. Just my dad's car now.

I went in through the garage and up the stairs. My dad met me at the top of the stairs. He was carrying a suitcase. I felt confused, didn't know he was headed on a business trip. My insides felt funny.

Where was he going?

"Hi," he said, setting the suitcase down.

My joy flip-flopped and fell in my stomach.

"I need you to hear me," he said. "I'm leaving and not coming back," screams thick in my head, what was he saying?

"I need you to tell the family I won't be coming back."

Still, I could say nothing. Why was he talking like this?

He tried to hug me. He was so sad, his eyes watery. This was hard for him. It was hard for me. Why was he going? My parents fought but was this the end? Was this the way?

He picked up his suitcase and walked down the stairs. I watched from the front window as he got into his car. I watched him back up and out of my life that day.

I paced down the hall. My joy to be alive, my peace from the weekend was lost, gone, like my dad. I went and curled up on my parents' bed and wept.

Now, I wasn't on my parents' bed, there hadn't been a parent's bed even with all of us living there. I used to think of the word 'together.' To-get-her, if only he knew how to do that, then maybe all the yelling, the fights, the sneaking

around behind each other would dissolve.
Into just being together.

To-get- her

To -get- her, together
we used to be a family playing games
on a cardboard table
with parents and children capable
of staying the night.
Now the hall is empty, the carpet no longer
worn, the ragged thoughts of early adolescence
I just want back.
Stubborn situations
unwilling to resolve the differences.
I waited in an empty family room
with no one to start the game.
I rolled the dice,
decided it was a gamble this life,
and went to do extreme makeovers,
a childish tantrum
of destruction.

I rubbed my eyes. I was still upon the pink comforter in a room amid the Green Mountains. At Alyssum, the rain had stopped, the fog was lifting. Sunshine was coming out. Maybe today was going to be a good day to say goodbye to so much more. Possibilities were creating. I went to the rocking chair in the room and picked up my sewing.

I knitted as I rocked. I soothed my body to the rhythm of the movement. I stayed present to my hands moving, needles clicking together, knitting the yarn into a pattern.

I looked out at the steep mountainside that went so

high, beginning at the edge of the house. Just beyond the river, it rose so high. I imagined black bears with cubs, deer with fawn, all coming to drink at the flowing water. I let my eyes paint an image, watched it play out.

All I wanted was to write these feelings out, release the pain, squeeze it up into a ball, or a rock, and fling it away for good, until bad feelings about myself fell to nothingness. At Alyssum, there was a computer to share, and so when it was available, I began to write this, my story. I realized that nature was healing me, the environment, a safe place to relieve my aches, my hurts, my PTSD and anxiety.

I also needed prayer life to grow. Always prayer life showed something deeper than just my little life. It was how I had met my husband. We shared a faith which helped us through such sad times and enriched such good times. God was all around our lives and it was so easy to breathe when focused on that.

Twenty-four years ago, a marriage, and three boys through the years, and still such depth to our lives. Such joy when we were together. Jim had always been there with me when I needed him. He was quick to hold tight to me when I needed that, and ready to defend me.

I remembered when I first thought I was pregnant. In my dorm room in college, eighteen and throwing up breakfast. I had walked down the hill to Planned Parenthood and taken the test.

I was worried that Jim might not want to stay with me, even though he had given me a diamond-like ring as a someday real ring months before. I was worried that he might not want to stay with this baby. I was scared. A nurse took me to a room and said little to comfort.

The room was so white, harshly lit. I felt so down, so gray, beaten. I waited for the nurse to come back. No phones then, no tablets to read on, just the waiting and old magazines.

The nurse was back, didn't look at me.

"How soon do you want to abort?" The nurse was looking at her papers.

There was no pregnancy news. No possible congratulations in her voice. The nurse kept her eyes away, averted from me. Simply there to cut this part of my life out and flush it away.

No.

I said nothing but stood and walked out of the room. Just left.

I went to Jim. Brought him the scared mixed up dilemma and waited. He trembled as he took me in his strong arms, held me, listened to me speak.

"We are having a baby," he said simply.

And that baby saved my life. Both of us.

I loved that baby boy so much. I fed and clothed and played with my first son. I taught him joy. He gave it right back.

On the long days my husband worked, I would take my toddler down to the lake to watch the ducks. Jimmy liked to chase them and watch as they slipped into the water away from his ever-sticky fingers. I didn't think he would know what to do if he actually caught hold of one of them. That didn't stop him though.

I delighted in my son's antics by Lake Champlain. He would toddle about and I would follow, overseeing his safety, encouraging him to explore, to live. He would reach his arms out and I would scoop him up, hold him close with kisses as we waited for my husband, his daddy.

My husband worked long hours. He had taken a hard job at a meat plant because it was the first job with insurance. He worked hard, bone-tiring days. He was always the last to leave.

After four years, he was managing the beef plant and doing well for us, his family at 24. I loved him so much for his strength, his determination to take care of us.

"We're coming for you," a male voice. Another neighbor.

"You deserve to die."

I looked down at my little boy. I still possessed happiness with my small family. The idea of settling down. That's what it felt like to be part of a family, even with the neighbors inside me. The dark thoughts exposed from my trauma, my pain. My fear.

I brushed little Jimmy's cheek. This little adoration, my own four-year old prayer created out of our love. I cared so much about him. This little guy with the squatting dances to Bruce Springsteen. That smile while his feet slid the cozy coupe car across the brown rug of our old apartment, and then our old tiny house on Weaver Street. The child who once had sticky fingers and palms coated with peanut butter that tried to slide a sandwich into the VHS deck so he could dance again. That beauty beyond the negative noise. Soon to have another.

The Calling

The noise is loud
drowns me in the liquid
desperation I
cling to. Those tears wiping
the stain of evil
fought in my
mind.

I look to my child, innocence
given to me to tend,
to take on, to wrap my real wonderfulness into all of
his being.

CHAPTER EIGHT

Back at the retreat, I continued to knit. I looked at the shelf where I had placed a knitted mat and a felted mushroom house I had made. It was a fairy house for I still liked to dream. I had piled river rocks about the shelf so that Michael, my third son, could find them when he visited. A simple surprise I could deliver.

So I could smile as his eyes went wide with the discovery. Oh how I missed my family. Missed the rhythm of our time together. I wished I could step into that small world I had made there on the shelf, and play like my childhood self about the rocks.

Lost in thought, I rocked on.

I was alone on top of a mountain. Not alone, just not with my family. I was in a house by the riverside.

I wanted to go to the river and release some more stored up emotion. I was learning to sit with my mood. Karen helped so much. She listened, confirmed my strength as we sat by the river. I let my self take me to the raw pain. To feel the feelings and then to detach from the pain here at the retreat house, the fields, the river that ever flowed.

For it was a healing retreat that I was on. A place to put away past pain and to grow so I could go back home to live in the moment.

Today, Karen had helped me release some of the stored up baggage I held onto for some reason. I had been heard, and it felt good to have someone hear my words. To really feel like I mattered. Karen shook back her long white hair and really looked at me while I talked. She too had been through hardships. She too had shared and let go of her stored up baggage.

It had been a while since I cared about myself. It had been a long time since I hadn't focused on the angry neighbors. They seemed to break through and find me, trap me into ignoring my needs. Made me think less of myself.

I didn't think I believed in myself but I wanted to start. There was no getting past it if I wanted to fully heal.

And I had tried many procedures to lift my depression.

After Andy, my second son turned two, I agreed to have ECT. Electro-Convulsive Therapy. The doctors shocked my brain on both sides.

They hadn't told me about the coldness rushing through my veins. The desire to run away so vivid, revealed only to the nurses who just patted my hand but wouldn't let me up. Didn't tell me that after I woke up from the procedure I would lose some of my memory. Still, I had treatments for a course of two weeks. Each day, I would lie flat on the table, unable to move, tears sliding from my eyes, trailing down my neck until I went up and over, then out in the anesthesia.

They put an IV in my arm each morning, then after the procedure, would forget to monitor me in my confusion. I would wake up back on the psychiatric floor, from the procedure, tired, groggy, disoriented. One morning in the bathroom, I looked at my arm and wondered what was sticking out of me.

I pulled at the IV and it came out in my hand. Blood poured down my arm and I watched it, detached. I walked down the hall and a nurse noticed and came running. The nurse asked why I had taken the IV out but I had no memory of doing so.

I didn't feel anything. Couldn't.

Tears would fall from my eyes but I wasn't connected to them. I was lost in a bubble.

Medicine blocked out the world while ECT tried to reset my way of thinking.

It had helped some. I was less depressed, but smells brought me right back to the procedure. Right back to the table where I was frozen, unable to move with a plastic oxygen mask on, and then that cold running into my veins as the medicine was put into the IV. And then finally, the feeling of fading into nothing.

That still haunted me. Drifting off into an endless void of nothing. Unable to control my world.

Help

They said this method
could cure madness,
the dilemma of
dying. Instead
of listening
they patted my arm,
said I couldn't
get up, made me fall
backwards into the abyss
of nothing to lose
memories with the sad,
the crazy chaos in my head.
Was I really given a choice?

Years later as my depression worsened again, I went back and had another series of ECT. But the process was too much, reliving the steps, crying, unable to get beyond what they were doing to me.

They only shocked one side of my brain so I wouldn't lose another year of memories like before.

I could recall being frozen on the table, tears running into my ears, asking the doctors to stop the procedure, let me up.

A nurse had patted my arm. It didn't help. I couldn't move. No one really heard me.

"Please put me out fast, I can't take this."

My anxiety was so large, I had so much pain from the way they treated me that I couldn't deal with what was happening. All the decisions made without hearing me.

I hated the icy feeling in my veins as the medicine traveled up my arm, the plastic smell of the oxygen mask again. Then, feeling like I was tipping over backwards and falling through the bed into nothingness.

The last treatments really didn't help. My mind was too traumatized. All I felt was anxiety. Too many times in my life I hadn't been in control of what happened. This had been too much for me.

Back at Alyssum, I wanted a cigarette. Wanted to blow out smoke and not worry that I was disappointing family, that I could decide for myself what to do. A pause. An intake of breath. I kept on writing. Kept right on writing.

What's Wrong?

I want to press
my lips against the white,
inhale my mindful obedience
to the smoke.
Drift on the current trends
of peace,
float through the thick mist
of indecision and blow out,
exhale my inhibition,
my slow tortured willfulness to survive.

Just let me slowly steal the tar from this,
stick the pain on a
limited shelf life.
Preserve nothing
that reminds me
of the trauma I hear every day.

It was too late to make church. I hoped that I could be there on Sunday. I missed Communion. I watched my handwriting sprawl over the page, really messy. Sarah, my red-haired roommate was on the computer. It was easier to write than to print, so I kept at it.

I wished I had a computer that I could use all the time. It was hard to write and to form words with a pen when there wasn't a keyboard available.

Tonight, I painted ladybugs on rocks. Cindy, another peer support worker, showed me how to make the rocks look like ladybugs. It was calming to dip the brushes into colors and turn the rocks into something so colorful. Cindy bent her short, dark hair over the table, carefully painting thin antennae onto the rock. It really looked good. I tried my hand at it too. My lines were wavy but I could tell that it was a red ladybug with black dots and an antenna.

Anxiety seemed to call on everyone in the house that night. Something in the air? Still foggy and wet outside, camping weather I called it, always wet and cold when we would camp.

It was getting dark and I thought of the coyotes outside and shivered. I heard they went to the river early in the morning, and again at dusk. I wanted to go down and see them, but not alone, no that would not be calming.

And so I kept to painting the rocks. I made a family of five ladybugs.

No message yet from Jim. God I missed him so. I knew what I needed to do. I needed to finish reliving my experiences. Tossing them all into the river for medicine would never be enough. I still had inside work to do.

One of my housemates made vanilla pudding chocolate chip muffins and we had all had one.

So delicious.

I remembered how I used to get the munchies after I drank and smoked. That's the time when the most pain was upon me. Shame, guilt, pain, fear, all mixed up. The worse it got, the more I drank and smoked as a young teenager. I was tempting the universe to stop the madness. It didn't.

I worked at Camp Tara during the summer I was sixteen. I was a camp counselor and way too young to be off making my own decisions. I had a car and the company of other counselors who knew the Colchester area. We went to parties between camp sessions. We drank too much, smoked too much, and drove when we should not have.

I recalled one night I had smoked hash with a boyfriend and then got behind the wheel. I wasn't thinking clearly, only setting out for my friends at a house nearby. I turned the key to my Chevette and drove down the camp road towards the party.

It was dark, I couldn't see very well. The road twisted and I swerved with it, over-extending my turns. I shouldn't have been driving. I drove slowly to compensate for the quick responses of the steering wheel.

Up ahead was a curve, and I slowed down even more. A brick wall came up in view. I slammed on the brakes. The car came to a suddeb stop just before it. I squeezed tight on the wheel, looked down at my lap, breathed in and out.

When I looked up, the brick wall was gone. Confused,

I got out of my car and walked to the side of the road. Where the brick wall had appeared, was the edge of a ravine. I had almost gone over the brink. If I hadn't seen the wall, I would have gone right over the side.

I tried to sober my thoughts, and tried to focus on being safe. I felt for a wooden cross that I wore beneath my shirt. I squeezed it for comfort, for delivering something that was looking out for me. I really wanted to be back home, wanted to end this reckless course. But the summer was just sliding into July and I had almost two months left at camp.

I got back in the car. I thanked God for the brick wall. I willed myself to pray a Hail Mary, and then I returned to camp. I had had enough of partying for the night.

When summer ended I was doing drugs most weekends. I liked the feeling of disappearing, not thinking of pain or fights or the dark thoughts that I had. At school I would sneak in the bathrooms and have a cigarette. I was hooked on them and couldn't get through the day without one. My father was back home but he stayed downstairs mostly when my mother was home. Mom worked second shift, she worked hard to buy things for us. My mother was so sad then. She seemed to want to hide from us. She was gone before we got home from school. I wondered what pain was stored up inside my mom. I wished I felt like I could go to her, tell her my pain, talk to her.

I remembered when nightmares started for me at thirteen. My mother would come home late from work and I would still be up, afraid to sleep. She would lie beside me on my bed and rub my hair. It was a tender moment that I savored.

I recalled that I had watched *The Exorcist* on a tiny television in the kitchen one night when I couldn't sleep. I watched that scary thriller in black and white, fear reaching out and taking hold of my thoughts.

The next morning, I awoke with my bed shaking in my room. I immediately assumed that I was being possessed by some horror. I didn't realize that there had been an earthquake tremor that shook lots of things. My nightmares continued and I had trouble sleeping. My mother was tired from work but still came in and held me. I clung to my mother in desperation. Tried to explain my pain in poems I posted on the back of my bedroom door. No one saw them. I was seventeen.

United

United to carve
the face of sin,
flesh of hell
Impitted,
sheds with one tear.

It had gotten worse. So, my parents sent me to a psychiatrist. I recalled going to the first appointment, my parents sitting on either side of me in the office. An older man, the doctor leaned across his desk and asked why I was upset.

I stared at his bald head and beard. His soft hands folded, elbows on the desk.

But, I had no words for him. I didn't know how to express the pain that I felt, the despair and loneliness that consumed me, the pain of alcohol coursing through the family not communicating with each other. I said little, prayed someone would find me, help me. My parents didn't send me back.

I tried to control my world with order. I straightened

rooms, lined up shoes in the living areas, kept cupboards closed, and I counted often, tried to breathe. I tried to make sense of life and the pain that I felt. The years passed. I had boyfriends, kissed and touched. I was a young girl looking for love. I was just looking in the wrong places.

After Camp Tara, when I was sixteen, I started going to parties at UVM. I drank and smoked. I was out of control, but didn't know it then. I had so many nights where I blacked out and didn't remember anything. I wanted not to think or be in the present. I had friends that went with me, friends that were searching for something inside, and drowning those thoughts with alcohol and drugs.

One night, I went out with a friend downtown. We had gotten a ride from another friend and were walking the streets of Burlington, high and looking for something to do.

A car pulled up next to us with two guys inside. One leaned out the window and asked if we knew how to get to UVM. My friend pointed the way.

"Could you just come with us? It would be a lot faster. We're headed to a party," the guy at the window said.

My friend got in the car right away. I didn't feel it was a great idea, but I wasn't going to let my friend drive off alone. I got in too.

They parked over near Gutterson Field House, the sports area of the university. My friend got in the front seat and started kissing the guy behind the wheel. I didn't want to watch so I got out of the car and went into the dorm. I walked through the kitchen and saw a group of guys and girls making a pizza. I laughed in my stoned stupor and tried to help them. They encouraged me as I added pepperoni to the unbaked crust.

I continued through the hall, winding through corridors until I was at my friend Tim's room. I knocked at the door and he opened it right up. I looked at him. He had short dark hair, dark eyes, and a smile on his face. He took my arm and led me inside.

I should have stayed with Tim. Should have curled up on his bed and spent the night. But, I remembered my friend out there with those guys and I worried about her. Tim was drinking and I had one with him.

I had known Tim from youth group retreats. We had written letters to each other after the retreats and had grown close. He was a good friend. But I had another friend out in the darkness that I needed to find.

I kissed Tim goodbye and went back out to the car. My friend was gone, one of the guys still sat in the car. He said my friend had gone off with the driver. So I got back in the car, sat next to this stranger, and tried to think soberly.

He kissed me and I pushed him away. I didn't want that. He kissed me again and this time I accepted it. I didn't want to be there. I wanted to run back and be with Tim. I wanted to know if my friend was okay. I squeezed my eyes shut and tried to sober up. I hated this moment but didn't know where my friend was or what she was doing. I wanted her to be okay, so I sat there with this stranger. He tried to kiss me again and I tensed up. He laughed and touched my hair. I wished my friend would hurry up and come back. I wanted to go home and sleep off a growing headache.

The guy was on top of me and my hands were clumsily trying to get him off. He persisted, pulled down my pants. I tried to get him off but he was too strong. I wished for this night to be over. I couldn't take it. Where was my friend? Tears fell down into my ears as he pushed into me. I cried the whole time, shaking my head, wishing I was home.

When he was done, he got off and went outside, lit a cigarette. My head was pounding as I pulled up my pants. This night was not what I had envisioned. I really hadn't had a plan, I just wished I was back in Tim's room, sleeping. I was worried about my friend though, had wondered if she would be okay.

She finally came back holding the driver's hand. They got into the car and the other guy got back in too. They drove us back to my house, my friend kissing the driver as I got out. I was going to be sick, and didn't look back as I made my way to my house.

Inside, I showered, tried to rid myself of the unclean thoughts and feelings. The soap and water poured over me, but didn't help. I felt like I was suffocating. I wished I knew what to do. I let the water run over me as I cried in its stream.

When I got back to my room, my friend was asleep on my waterbed. I climbed in next to her and let the soft waving motion lull me to sleep. Sleep. Sleep was what I needed. Back to childhood dreams on a hill with others, the soil, the ability to breathe, and dig into a new life.

Digging

I remember digging on the hill,
my fingernails black with the earth.
The soil sprinkling bits
of nature to cover our unity
beyond neighborhood kids.
My hands were beautiful in their darkness.
My surroundings consumed my fear,
kept me there
with the birds gathering,

the field mice scurrying,
the sun setting
while the birch trees' whiteness
contrasted with my new blending
of the outside.

    Back from my memories at Alyssum, I stretched out on the pink comforter. I looked out the window. It was no longer raining. I was no longer that little girl who was afraid. I thought to myself that I had been hurt. How I had cried, and cried, and wished I knew who to talk to about it.

    The men who had hurt me had used me as nothing. I heard their laughter in my head. Laughter that had come back whenever I listened to the neighbors. The neighbors were loud. The neighbors were the male voices I wished to turn off, make them disappear.

    I looked out my window and did not see the darkness, nor hear the coyotes. I was physically there amid the Green Mountains, but my mind was back to my troubled teens. That's what PTSD was like. Flashing back to past traumas. No longer certain what time it was, what place I was in.

    I was thinking about 1986. So many black outs, too little sense. I thought to the times I couldn't remember driving home, how it must have been God who had kept me and others safe on the road while I drove. Shame stained me, made me feel evil. I thought back to that troubled girl, sixteen-years old and a mess. There was one night worse than what I'd already been through, that troubled me still. I couldn't get it out of my head, the pain, the hurt, the feeling of being so alone in the world. 1986 was a bad year. I was lost in memory as my body rocked on the pink comforter at the retreat house in the Green Mountains.

CHAPTER NINE

We had driven to a college frat party and were greeted at the door with a hug and a drink.

My friend Kim had drifted through the small crowd, smiling, laughing at jokes. I followed her through the frat house, drinking along the way. We wandered together, through the crowd, chatting, laughing, and drinking more.

Kim wandered off to dance with someone while I watched. Kim swayed to the music that was playing. Her dark hair swaying with her. I stood and watched the people dancing, some kissing in corners. An arm went around my waist and I was pulled through the room.

"Come with me," a guy said, steering me through the living room, through the kitchen, down a hall.

I looked back and saw Kim doing shots on the edge of the couch.

The guy led me to a room lined with bookshelves. We were alone in a dark room. I didn't like it, but didn't know how to politely leave.

He picked up a water bong and held it out to me. I knew it was a bad idea, knew I should be back near Kim. I took it and inhaled away all sense.

It was strong, and I felt like I was really tall. The guy took a hit and then started taking my clothes off, dancing me around.

"No, don't do that," I said, pulling away. My head was swimming, I felt all fuzzy, detached from my body. Not this time.

He was strong too. He smiled and sidled up to me. He held me in his arms and then pulled down my pants. I tried to pull them up but couldn't find them. He was taking my underwear down too.

I got a finger in the underwear and tried to pull them back up. He pushed me down to the ground.

His hands were under my shirt, I twisted away but he pinned me down. My shirt tore, and he grabbed at my breasts. He hurt me. I was bruised. My head hit the floor, I still felt dizzy. I couldn't think, couldn't get him off me. I screamed and he muffled it. I bit his fingers and he laughed, held me down. He was strong and I felt like I was being pulled like taffy on a machine. Stretching away from reality.

"Please stop," I said, unable to say anymore. He was pushing himself into me now. I could feel him and it was terrible. I tried to resist him, but my hands didn't work. I realized they were over my head, gripped in one of his hands.

My back hurt as he pushed inside me. The floor was hard and my head banged again, and again, against the floor. I needed to move, but couldn't. Tears carved my face in wet lines. This wasn't right. I tried to lose myself in the drug and drink, but I was sobering up now and fear was settling in. Would he ever be done?

He pushed off, leaving me on the floor. He pulled his pants up and walked over to a mirror. I curled up with my knees against my chest. I hurt, but couldn't feel. I wanted to run, but couldn't move. I felt bruised, beaten up. I was gonna be sick. What was wrong with me? I wanted to be anywhere but here, in this awful room.

I pressed my hands down my legs. They felt weak, but I found my pants and underwear, and pulled them up. My shirt was ripped down one side. I didn't care, I wanted out of there.

I was going to be sick. I sat up and puked right there on the floor.

The guy looked at me and shook his head.

I wiped drool off my lips, felt the pain in my back.

Everything was moving slowly and I couldn't seem to move fast enough.

There was something I still had to do. What was it? I had my keys in hand when I remembered Kim.

I needed help, no one was around. I feared him, but wanted to find Kim. I couldn't get the words out. I walked out of the room while he was brushing his hair. I didn't care how I looked. Just wanted to be home in bed.

The place was quieter. People curled up in corners, a lot of people had cleared out. I walked through the rooms until I found her, passed out on a couch upstairs in a bed-room.

I tried to rouse my friend but she was out of it. I couldn't lift her without help. I needed to get her to my car. Had anyone hurt her? I should have been there to make sure no one had.

I went back downstairs and found the guy, the horrible guy who had taken a part of me that years later I would still be struggling to get back. I found him in the kitchen.

"Could you help me get my friend to my car?" The guy looked at me. "Please, she's passed out, and I need to go."

The guy agreed and went and got another to help him bring her out to the car. I was outside breathing in the cool Fall air. I was scared. I wanted to run. I waited for Kim.

The guys carried Kim out. One had her head in his hands, the other lugged her legs. They brought her to the backseat of my car. The guy that had hurt me, had broken me, and had taken a part of me, stood close once Kim was in the back.

"You could bring her home and come back," he whispered.

Vomit taste in my mouth, I was going to be sick again. I puked by the car and without a word, got inside. I locked the door. Both guys laughed and walked back to the house.

Headlights and a prayer. I turned the car on. Let us make it home. I never knew how we made it. Somehow, God had saved me from hurting anyone else.

I took Kim home with me because no one would bother us there. She barely woke up, but was able to get inside and into my bed.

I was crying, my chest heaving as I took off my clothes in the bathroom. My back and a leg was bruised. I stepped into the shower and let the water wash over me. I cried and let tears drain away until I felt nothing. I was lost in nothingness.

Empty

I am nothing, so far from my former self, a
companion with no map, no more destiny but
to fill the void inside.
Pain screams, aches shake me. I upend
my thoughts, drink the bitter mead, the
lager, from cheap plastic cups, while I
inhale more confusion, wager with the devil
by letting sense go.
Am I still just a husk of before?

1986 went away; now here I was at the retreat house still dealing with past pain.

And the neighbors were relentless. They harassed me so much.

"You'll never be good enough. You are evil. Jim is better off without you. You are worthless."

I shook my head, tried to find the calm, sincere voice of my love. He loved me so much.

He didn't believe the neighbors.

Back in the eighties, I would have drank or smoked away the raw pain. God, how I wanted a cig. Now, I had a list of prescribed drugs that were "approved." Uppers, downers, and in between, sedation so I wouldn't scream. Uppers so I could function, downers again so I could sleep, antidepressants so I wouldn't cry all day. I was a dutiful patient, a dutiful soul. I swallowed it all.

I wished I knew how to scream. Cindy, a middle aged peer support worker, said it would be good to stand under a train bridge when a train went by, to just let go of my anger in a raging scream. Scream until I no longer had a voice to shout out, to expend all the stress and energy that consumed me. I wished again that I knew how to scream. I screamed a lot in my head, but that just increased my anxiety, and did not relieve me.

Jim had always tried to get me to scream, "It's Friday night!" but I wasn't able to. He would take me in the car, play loud rock, roll down his window, and let loose with that scream, "It's Friday night!" I loved that he was trying to help, but my anxiety was still too high.

At Alyssum now, I thought I heard a coyote. Maybe by the river. Maybe just in my head. Maybe it was out hunting. Maybe I wished I was out there howling with it. I blew out imagined smoke, wished for a cigarette, then went to bed.

CHAPTER TEN

My friend sent me Psalm 23:
> The Lord is my shepherd, I lack nothing.
> He maketh me lie down in green pastures.
> He leads me beside quiet waters.
> He refreshes my soul.
> He guides me along the right path for his name's sake.

Well, I was certainly in a beautiful space here at the retreat house. I had just come in from the back deck where I had sat in the sun. I had focused on my breath, in and out, thinking only of the sun on my arms and face, the yellow spots of the sun behind my eyelids as I lay there, eyes closed. Birds entered the moment, chirping songs to fill the wind. And the wind blew the music to me.

It had gotten too hot, so now I was inside. I felt tired. So much work today. So much exhaustion in letting the baggage go.

I prayed for strength from St. Teresa of Avila. Courage too, to keep up with my own writing as St. Teresa had kept to hers.

I prayed to the Little Flower, St. Theresa, to see beauty in myself and my surroundings. I prayed to her for the knowledge to breathe in and out, to be still and calm in my place in life.

I prayed to Mary, Mother of God. One mother to another. I asked for confidence to keep doing the work so that I could go back to being the mother my children needed. I prayed to her for determination to continue my work.

For I had answered the call to try to become a saint and really wanted to learn how to do that. I so wanted to be in the arms of the Lord, to find that eternal peace. I had to find the beginnings of it here, so I would be ready to face the Lord.

I thought to my prayer life and knew it needed work, but I was at a place where I was growing. It felt right. I thought of Notre Dame De Vie and the House of Solitude. How wonderful and quiet it was in the retreat house up in Canada. Not a lot of neighbors. I could focus there on my breathing, my prayer life. I felt safe there. I was starting to feel safe here.

I prayed that the Holy Spirit would fill me with its wonder and understanding. I wanted to feel the path my life should take. I wanted to help fill the world with love for as many as I could. And of course for my family, whom I adored.

God made me, experiences shaped me, prayer grounded me, and my written words filled a deep need inside.

I looked down at Ladybug the dog, looking out to the mountains. The trees rocked in the gentleness of the day. It was okay to love the day. It was okay to love myself. I was here at this retreat house learning to breathe. I was learning to be. I was learning to love this girl who hurt so much. The one whose husband found so much joy to be with, and with whom I too wanted to feel joy. Thinking of my husband, I remembered the "almost" first kiss we shared.

We had been standing on the landing at my parents' house, so close but not touching. He was so different from the guys I knew. He wanted just to be with me, talk with me, laugh with me. No pressure, he wanted to listen to me. We were both seventeen, but it felt like a first moment for me. Like maybe this was how a seventeen was supposed to be treated. I felt like my pain had been pushed away, and I was back at the beginning, being with a boy for the first time.

Jim had leaned in, our bodies so close, not touching. I could feel his breath on me. This was so new. I wanted him to kiss me. To kiss, and to kiss me without laughing.

"Hey you two!" our good friend Todd had called from up the stairs. And the moment was lost. I was tingling, and almost felt like shaking. Something had happened. I was falling in love with someone who was falling for me too. It was the first moment I would always remember.

Oh, how I loved growing into adulthood with him.

My knitting sat beside me. My tablet void of new messages. A Diet Coke sat on the nightstand by my CPAP (continuous positive airway pressure therapy, a treatment for my sleep apnea). I closed my eyes and recalled the view of the outside. The trees scattered about the yard, the rolling hills that swelled up from the farmer's fields, bursting into flatness at the crest where the house stood. Yes, there was beauty in the world.

I had gone to the river and thrown rocks into the current. I had shouted curses to the air with Cindy who encouraged me, her short black hair blowing in the wind along with her loud booming voice. I had sworn softly as I tossed the rocks into the water making splashes.

Gathering courage from the heavy rocks, I raised my voice with each toss, each hurl into the water.

"Scream Jo!" Cindy raised her face to the sky, let out a whoop and flung a stone deep into the middle of the river. She howled and smiled at me. I threw my anger into the river and watched the wetness take it from me. I lifted another rock, tried to yell, more of a moan came out.

"Good start Jo!"

The rock left my hand and sailed out and away. I felt a stirring in my chest, a tickle wanting to be released. A need to be heard. Again and again, I scooped up the stones and let them slice through the air to crash into the water, breaking my resolve to hold everything inside.

Poem

Pain pushed into the cold water with the
plunging rocks tied to my emotions so deep. I
stirred, swelled, exploded into the air with my
voice, a shrill escape from lips left sealed too
long. I released my torment, a prison opened to
rage at my captors until my swears died back
to the moaning of my lament in the wind. Quiet
now as the water takes the sharp stones, the
insults, the heaviness from my soul.
And I am still alive.
Perhaps it was good to sizzle, to settle down on
the river rocks cried out now from the moment
of madness that has locked me up for ever so
long.

Drained from the demonstration, the power of the physical exertion, I turned to thoughts of my family. I reached out along the bank and picked up rocks, turning them in my hands. I collected flat rocks to paint with my little boy when he visited. He was five and I was going to show him how to paint ladybugs or whatever he wanted to paint on the river rocks. I would make his visit simple, filled with activity.

I felt purged and tired. A good tired. Like my body was pulsing in and out. Reforming from the regression, the aggression, the release. I breathed in and out. I savored each intake, each out breath. I looked at my housemate.

She skipped rocks, almost eight skips with one rock. I almost made one fly across to the other riverbank.

There on the bank, with all those rocks, we shared pain. With Cindy's guidance, we had felt the rawness of each ache, released the abuse we still carried as a wound to the current. Gave it to the river to wash it away.

I breathed deeply. Outside, it smelled like childhood to me. Smelled like pine, water, flowers, and dirt. Smelled like racing through a field holding hands with a friend. Like the days with Jen, my childhood friend, picnics together on the hill, making chocolate chip cookies by the red, land line telephone in the kitchen, sleeping and dreaming and wishing together as children. I inhaled deeply as the pain in my chest became lighter.

And the river took it all. I watched my sadness float off in the current. I could keep doing this. I could keep taking out the baggage that made me dislike myself so much. I could be strong like the running current.

The neighbors were loud again. They shouted at me, told me I was no good. I shook my head to shake them off. They whispered hate in my ears. I lifted a stone from the shore and tossed it into the water. The stone made a loud plopping as it sunk to the bottom of the river. I defied the neighbors' words with another shake of my head. I was in control. I was here, outside, by the river.

I slipped my shoes off and felt the warmth of the smooth rocks beneath me. I wiggled my toes against the worn rocks. I breathed in the smell of the weeds and the flowers by the edge of the banks, the manure on the farmer's fields.

I was here in Rochester living in the moment.

The neighbors left. I listened instead to the chirping insects, the current of the river against the rocks. I watched the sky so clear, my mind clearing more and more. And I wept for the beauty I wished I could become, wished I could believe in. And I tried to accept the beauty there by the running waters, on a hilltop in Vermont, that it was still possible to be me.

CHAPTER ELEVEN

In the morning, I woke to rain sliding down the window-panes again. I wanted it to be nice for my visit with Jim and Michael. I set out to get ready, showered, dressed, and then, since it was only 6 a.m., I went back to bed.

I scanned my email and found a morning note from my husband. He was on his way soon. He was as excited as I was for our meeting. I smiled thinking of him holding me close.

The clock dragged its arms around very slowly. I went out to the living room and worked at a puzzle with Karen. We talked about my writing, the rawness of my pain taken out on the white screen of the computer there.

I was in control of my environment. I was safe from harm and was taking care of myself. This was a safe place to finally let the trauma out, to be rid of the memories that seemed to keep me stuck in the past.

I had a cigarette. There, I said it. And there were more. I couldn't seem to stop. In and out, one puff and another. I would have to stop. It wasn't helping. I wasn't really a smoker anymore, and was unsure why I let myself talk me into having one.

I still felt broken, used up. I looked at the clock, almost time for their visit. Would they be happy to see me?

A knock at the door and it was them. I made my way to the doorway and watched as Karen let them in. Such smiles! It tore at my heart, I loved them so much. They climbed inside and hugged me tight.

Karen asked Jim if he wanted a coffee and he was glad to accept. We sat in the living room and my little boy bubbled on about his days. I fell back to the natural rhythm of listening to him, enjoying his peaceful life. My eyes kept glancing at my husband, taking him in. God knew I loved him.

I told Michael about painting ladybugs on rocks and we went right to painting the first red coat on one. He was so excited and smiled so sincerely that I was happy just to be there, adding color on the stones.

With the rocks set to dry, we went for a walk to the river. The sun had come out and it was a good break from the gray. We followed past the garden, down the hill, and towards the farmer's barn.

Young cows mooed at us, thinking we had come to bring them food. We walked past, mooing back at them. We zig-zagged through the field, avoiding the manure piles, and then on to the side path. Jim and I walked, our little guy between us.

My dear husband smiled at me as I caught him staring. I tried to smile back. We made our way over the rocks and down to the riverside. So peaceful down there. Such a beautiful scene.

The rocks were scattered as if a child had emptied their toy box on the shore. All the jumbled stone to hobble over and stand among as we looked at the river.

Farther down, were four geese. They honked at the disturbance of their meeting. My little boy ran to the edge of the water and began throwing rocks into the stream. My husband skipped rocks across the top of the water. I stood back, watching my boys, my life.

The geese were honking as they came in to alight from another direction. Four flew over just a few feet from the tops of our heads and then landed in the water. There was more honking as the geese all got acquainted and squawked because of us in their midst.

I watched them with my husband. He came up behind and put his arms around my waist and it felt so good. I felt like falling into the water, and floating away on the current with my love. How much I longed to be with him always.

Life

Life could be this simple,
tossing rocks with a family,
laughing at the way the water
swirls up over the dropped stones.
The way the bubbles churn up
in whiteness cresting
the surface before us.
A happiness with the arc of a stone in air,
a smile for the sport, all by the river,
two boys with their girl.
The way the sun lightened their mood,
a brush of warmth on
cheeks, living in this very moment.

Sadness crept in as I turned and kissed him. I didn't want it to end. My youngest came up to us and pushed his way in between. I bent down and set to digging in the sand and water, making mud stew with the shovel and pail they had brought. Jim and Michael sat with me on the stones and together we played in the oozy, muddy bank, Michael all smiles.

After what seemed an instant but was probably an hour, we turned back and went up the way we had come. The cows were now eating and less mooing came from them, but not from us. We laughed as we all held hands and made our way back to the house. Stolen moments of normalcy.

I signed myself out and the three of us made our way over the mountain to Randolph. We passed some time shopping, wandered in and out of a few shops, and then brought lunch back to the house.

We ate together in the dining room where the ladybug rocks were drying. It was time to add the black lines and dots, and the white eyes. Michael was so excited to be painting with me.

I swallowed a large dose of guilt from my illness as I helped him coat the rocks.

Before it seemed to begin, the day was closing in on our meeting. Tears stained my cheeks as I pressed myself to resist them. Michael sobbed into my chest. I hugged him tight and looked at my husband. He tried to keep himself composed for the sake of our youngest son.

I hugged tight, clinging to the man I loved, breathed in his scent, let it wash through my memory, like the beautiful gift he left me, the sweet balloons back in my bedroom. And then one more hug to the crying boy, and they were out the door, gone from my sight.

I walked to my room with the pink comforter and wept, and wept until I slept.

That evening was the other housemate's last night and it was sad to think about her leaving. She had been a reassuring voice, another going through a shared pain. Another mother without her babies. I didn't really know her. Didn't open up and share with her my struggle, but I saw a younger version of me, a lost mom without her family.

We watched, mindless as zombies, sitting to eat popcorn seasoned with butter, salt, and pepper. A lot of pepper, but it was good. Allysa, the staff member on call, had made it to cheer us.

Then, I went to bed, passing the time away until morning when I would have another note from my husband. I shivered away my sadness, buried myself under the blankets, hooked on my CPAP, and faded away to sleep.

A happy memory: Christmas morning with all of my boys home. All three were there to wake up and share in the festivities. My husband there, grinning with me, as we watched our boys open small tokens of our love for them. The tree lit up, the gold and white wrapped and twinkled on the pine branches. A beautiful gift I could take out to remember and hold on to, remembering the created joy.

CHAPTER TWELVE

Mother's Day. No children to talk to, or to run up to me to share the day with. No wilting dandelions in small fists, no sugar-coated smiles to kiss. I went to church and prayed. I sat alone in a pew, with families about me. I prayed the rosary before Mass. Prayed for my heart to heal and for the neighbors to finally leave for good.

Roots and All

I like the flowers
with the roots still attached, the ones
my children bring me.
I like the soil that blackens
my hands as they hand me
them breathless with glee.
And though from my pots
my flowers grow more
without that trickle of dirt,
I still like the ones with the roots
still attached, that
sprinkle their dust on my shirt.

The noise in my head laughed at my thoughts, snarled in my ears, called me stupid. I prayed to Mary, dear sweet Mother Mary for help.

And then Mass started. I fell into its moment, stayed with Jesus up there on the mountaintop, singing and praying and then taking Jesus into myself. I swallowed Him in, swallowed up His love, so hungry for it.

Dear Lord

I take you inside my very being, swallowing
your goodness into me, help me return to my
family.
Bring me peace. Bring me peace.
Bring me from the painful path
I stumble down trying to reach your direction.
A light in the darkness, a plan for the ache.
Feed me.

Then it was over, and I was being picked up and
brought back to the house. I called my husband and we
talked. He wished me a happy day.

It had been a long day, rainy and then sunny, and then
rainy, and sunny again, as if this day too couldn't quite
make a decision. I had taken a ride to Randolph with Agh,
another peer support person. I brought back felt and had
set to making some felt food for Michael's play kitchen at
home. I made bacon and eggs and toast with Velcro-at-
tached butter pats. It was something to pass the time.

After the other housemate left, the house felt bigger
without her voice. I missed that voice. We exchanged numbers, wanted to get our kids together. Wanted to recon-
nect. I wondered if I would ever see her again.

I looked out to the mountains, ever still. The trees
all wrapped about the curve near me and formed a C for
compassion. I was filled with compassion for friends and
family, I was good enough.

Allysa came and brought some cigarettes with her. We
sat by the fire pit smoking them, releasing more pain. How
could one have so much hurt still left inside? I didn't know,

just that there it was. We inhaled and flicked the butts into the ashes of the burning wood.

Ladybug sat by my side, and I rubbed her fur, feeling its softness. I missed my family.

I messed myself up even further with the prescribed medications. One medicine had harmed my pancreas. Now, I was dependent on insulin. Others had left me drooling, sleepy, tired, anxious, irritable, the list went on. I had taken dozens of different medications over the years.

I thought about which ones I was on now. They didn't make the neighbors go away but kept them manageable. I liked my psychiatrist and my case manager. They believed in me. I stroked Ladybug's back and tossed a cigarette into the fire pit. Allysa didn't say anything, just sat with me in a comfortable silence.

I thought of the times when silence was hurtful, when I couldn't stand up for myself, make myself be heard, so I kept it all inside. I would scream in my head, but not want to make a sound outside of myself. Fear of loudness, fear of shouting, fear of screaming, left me quiet and subdued.

Here at the retreat house, I was learning to speak up. I was facing the fears and frustrations, my lack of understanding of the neighbors. I was trying to find peace in my mind. The neighbors laughed at me and made me feel pitiful. I shrank back from the noise, the threats, the constant buzzing of voices. I lit another cigarette and watched the fire.

My parents had fought a lot when I was a teenager. My mom worked second shift and my father worked days. When they came together at night, there were fights, and insults, and fear rushing from their mouths.

I used to wish I could go to my godmother's house and talk to her, have her listen to my pain. It hurt so much in my chest. I never did though, afraid to bother another. I used to wish I could put my head on my godmother's lap and have it gently rubbed. Rub away the headaches and heartaches. Outside of my godmother's home, grape vines grew in an arch. I used to walk through them into my own imagined seclusion. The vines' brown branches grew together and I would walk beneath them looking at the grapes as they appeared and ripened. I used to wish there were more places without harshness or sadness that I could live in, a place to hide from the spectacles that adults created.

Now as a woman, I wished I had gone into my parent's room screaming, shouting, making them stop hurting our family. All the tension-filled days were much worse than if they had simply divorced and left us children out of the hurt.

Instead, I clung to drink and drugs, finding my way to places where I could hide from all the noise in my life. I was afraid of the yelling, hated the way it made me feel so alone and unsure. And I had found other ways, but they were self-destructive.

I thought back to the times I never wanted to go back home. A tenseness was in the air back home. An invisible thickness that penetrated every room, and caused my family to hide from one another.

One night, I drank too much and didn't want to go home, afraid of getting caught. I had been with a friend and we were way over the limit, so much that I knew I shouldn't drive. It was winter, snow banks piled high, ice layered over the pavement.

We had just come from a party at UVM and were sitting in my Chevette. Neither of us spoke. We were tired and neither of us wanted to go home. So, we decided to sleep in the car overnight. I had a blanket in the back and we got it out and spread it over our coats, our breath coming out in steamy puffs.

It was cold in the car but we were warm from the drink. We curled up next to one another and slept off the alcohol. We had been foolish to sleep like that, I now thought. But we had woken up in the morning and driven home as if it was normal to spend the night outside in winter. Another save from a higher power? I wondered how many times the grace of God had intervened and helped me through uncertain times. More than I could count.

At home, my mother's parents came to stay with us for awhile. My grandmother was sick with a mental illness and my grandfather was dying of emphysema. Grandpa got to use my bedroom and my grandmother got to use my youngest brother's bedroom. The two of us kids slept on the couch in the living room. Our mother worked second shift, our older brother and sister were gone to friends' houses most of the time, and our dad lived downstairs.

I remember coming home from school not knowing what I would find. My grandmother would race down the hall and point a finger at me. She would talk in a soft voice, blame me and my mother. Always my mother. That angered me. When all I wanted was to get my field hockey uniform, grab my stick out of the closet, and escape like the rest of my family.

I would squeeze by my grandmother and knock on my bedroom door. There on a hospital bed, where my own bed used to be, lay my grandfather. Oxygen attached to his nose, he would reach out a hand. I never wanted to touch it, far too soft and worn. Not like the hands he had before when he would take us out to discover the hills behind his home in Bakersfield. Back then, his hands had been rough and scarred. Now they were limp and yellow. I would hurry, and smile, and get my field hockey uniform and then race back out.

My grandmother had the habit of wandering aimlessly around the upstairs, but never downstairs where my dad stayed. My father was back in the house, but he was reserved. I knew the strain between my parents. They just couldn't seem to find their way back to each other. They were too far away from each other, and I wished they would make a decision to either work things out or divorce.

Many of my friends' parents were splitting up. No one seemed to have a solid family life, at least none that I knew.

On days when there were no practices, I raced to the hill until the sun went down. I would shimmy up a tree and watch the world from up there. I would bring journals, and write, up on the hill, with legs dangling from a pine tree. The quiet stirrings of rabbits, and moles, and squirrels interested me, and I wrote about them. I breathed in and out with the wind tracing me with pine scent, with sap on my fingers sticking to my pencil. The sap was perfect to attach the pencil to my hand, to keep it up there with me in the tree. I loved the smell of the sap, the childhood aroma it conjured. There was perfection away from the loudness, the fear, and the loneliness.

I would close my journal and push it into the back side of my pants. Then, I'd climb down from the pine tree and curl up against the trunk. I would open up the case that held my vintage flute and I would play among the hill's own sounds. Oh, I was never really good at playing, but I would dance my fingers across the keys, stopping to sing a made-up verse, and then dance fingers onto the metal. I would laugh at wrong notes plucked by sticky fingers.

Those times, I didn't need to get high. Didn't need to be away from myself and my thoughts. I was on the hill behind my house where childhood memories welcomed me. I could think clearly, play my flute, just be by myself in the outdoors. It was a rare treat.

Thinking about that, made me recall when I first met my husband. We were at a retreat at Rockpoint behind Burlington High School. He was leaning against a window, his chair rocked back and I bounced over to introduced myself. After that, we saw each other occasionally when I wasn't using drugs, just being with church friends who didn't need to hide from themselves. We had been working on a retreat weekend together. I didn't need drink or drugs with my church friends, and Jim became one of them. When the retreat was over, we would all gather on weekends and hang out, talking, walking, just being in the moment, usually at a beach.

There were dances where I felt alive with the possibilities of being permanently happy within my mind. I would laugh and spin and dance. And Jim was there. The day after graduation, we started spending time together. I reached up one night and squeezed his hand when we were in a back-rub chain. And he had squeezed right back. I stopped doing drugs, stopped drinking. I spent my free time with Jim and his friends. It was a different experience. It felt good.

The summer kept us busy with work, and with play in the evenings. We went to beaches and had fires, swam, walked the shore with a gang of kids, all just spending time hanging out with each other. We'd rush off in the dark when a fireman would walk onto the beach, pull out his hat and stick it on his head. We'd laugh, run to our cars, find another deserted beach.

And we talked. Talked of little things and the big question of what we would do with our lives. College was coming in the fall for all of us and we were eager to start new lives.

I remembered walking at Leddy Beach with Jim. He had asked me where I thought our relationship was going now that summer was coming to an end. We were quiet together as we walked.

I turned to him and simply said, "I love you, but that's just me."

And he had loved me more for saying that. We continued our relationship, savoring the remaining days and nights we could spend with one another. Always, we wished we could sleep together side-by-side and not have to worry about rules and others' opinions, just be up close to one another and feel each other's closeness pressed into one another. We always joked about finding a small cabin like the ones we passed by the side of the road, where we could find comfort in each others arms.

His Scent

I breathe in his scent,
the leftover fragrance on my
sweater once pressed against his chest.
I hold the wool to my face
as I curl on my bed, rocking on
the waves of the heated water below me.
The thought of him
beside me, holding me,
me holding him right back, the yearning
to never be apart,
our hearts pulsing,

our breaths breathless as
we break away,
leaves me wanting.
I mourn the moments spent alone.

Some nights Jim would spend the night at my house. My mother would come home and set up a cot in my brother's room and he would sleep in the room right next door. He would hold my hand until I went to sleep, and then he would go rest in the other room. I loved that he wanted to be with me, help me find peace.

I blinked back to the fire pit. So many little things that made up my psyche. So many times I wished I could have done the better thing. On my high school graduation night, I told a friend that I would take care of her while she drank. I remembered my friend slipping away and when I went to find her, I discovered that she was being forced to have sex. My friend was crying, drunk, so upset. I thought back to the times that I had been hurt and beat myself up, guilty for not being there to watch her like I said I would.

I tossed my cigarette into the fire. Watched the flames consume the stub, wished sometimes that I would simply burn away. But I had more good times than bad. I just had to work to remember the good things.

I thought about my three boys and my husband. They loved me for being me. I thought of family and friends who believed in me, encouraged me to write. I had published two books of poetry and won a small creative writing contest. I had helped people with my second book of poetry.

I remembered giving a speech at the capitol where I then sold some of my books. A man in suspenders and a flannel shirt came up to me. He had a bushy beard and white hair.

He looked quite old.

"Well, I bought your book," he began. "I have a son who has schizophrenia and I went to his house and gave him the book. My son pushed it aside and I didn't think anything of it. Well, a week later he called me and asked me to come over to his place. When I went there, he told me he had read your book and he shared with me the poems that felt like he was talking, like they were his words on how he was feeling. We talked for the first time about his illness, talked in a way we hadn't in a very long time. I want to thank you for that."

Then, he smiled and slipped away into the crowd.

I felt proud to have helped someone be able to bridge the barrier between illness and recovery which always began with sharing. I had been sharing this week at the retreat house, letting my words carry me whereever they went. I was finding my voice and it felt good. I stroked Ladybug again.

I had given speeches to fund the book project. Doctors, business leaders, people who wanted to help me reduce stigma about having a mental illness helped. When the book was published in 2002, I was nominated for Vermont State Poet. My eldest son wrote an essay about how proud he was of his mother, how he just knew I would win.

I smiled thinking of that, of my sons. They always made me feel so right. I recalled taking them to poetry readings, having them create their own words to share during the sessions.

I thought it was important for them to have a voice at a young age.

There had been one disappointing moment with my second book. I had come home to a voice message. Someone wished me dead, thought my book was too sad, told me

I was bad for writing it. Told me to be careful. The man then hung up.

It had shaken me, made me call the police to report it. I locked the door and stayed in the kitchen with the light on until my husband had come home. It always came back to that feeling of safety in my husband's arms. He was my rock, my home, my perfection. I was good enough for him. He always wanted to protect me, love me back. I loved him more for that.

I stood up and stretched. I wished I could feel good about myself and not let the neighbors weigh me down. They were quiet right now. I knew I had done some bad things in my teen years that I was not proud of. Things that had hurt me enough. Drinking, drugs, bad choices. But here I was years later, still living with the guilt and the pain, and not getting on with life. I had a family that loved me. That needed me. I needed them too. Maybe I could live with my symptoms. Live with bipolar and PTSD. And the neighbors. This week had been all about the trauma. Trying to put it away, drive it out of me. Maybe I could improve.

I headed inside with Ladybug. Allysa, a young support worker with braids down her back, followed. We went to make dinner.

We made salads and fried eggplant. It was so good. I was getting used to tasting my food, small bites. I couldn't wait to go home and cook again. Cook for my family.

I wanted the pain to stop hurting in my chest. Oh yeah, it was time to take medicine. I got up and went to swallow away some of the hurt.

CHAPTER THIRTEEN

I woke in the morning ready to go home. I wrapped the idea around me and went to talk to Cindy. I had all these points about my homesickness, my need to be with my family, duties to reclaim.

We talked about my need to control everything. The way I tried to do all the things that needed doing around the house and for my family's lives. It was a new perspective. I was asked to think about spending two more days writing and talking. I relented, gave in as it seemed like a good idea, and went outside.

It was cold, winter back in the air. I huddled in the one sweater I had brought. It was supposed to be spring, but up here in the mountains, it was colder than the Champlain Valley I lived in. So much for spring right now. But the mountains hailed their own beauty. They slipped into my thoughts, their prettiness, their boldness as their green cover spread. I breathed deeply in the magnificence.

I was going to be okay. I was going to be more than that. I was going to find myself able to face the neighbors.

The neighbors laughed at me. They were in control, they wanted me to fear. I shook my head, raised a hand, and said, "No, let me go."

I turned my back to the noise they made. Turned from their hoots, sneers, and hot anger. I walked back inside, the door closing on the neighbors. They were still out there, but I was not going to listen to their tirade now.

I went and sat in a chair, looked down at Ladybug who was curled up on a dog bed. She looked like fluffiness, like something to rub, something to breathe in, of simple needs being met. I would try that too. I reached down and comforted myself through the touch of her fur, her softness.

I looked out at a squirrel racing past the French doors that led outside from the dining room. The squirrel made quick, jerky movements, always on alert. I was not going to be like that. I inhaled and let it all out. Then, I went to call my husband to tell him I was staying two more days.

I walked down the hall to the room I was using and lay on the pink comforter. The sun was full and brightly lit the room. I looked out at the grassy yard, watched another squirrel gather nuts, and tried to stay in the moment. My thoughts turned to the many retreats and hospitals I had been in.

Over thirty times I had been locked away for my safety. I had hidden away from the angry neighbors, curled up on so many different beds over the years. And still I had not found reprieve from the harassment of the noise.

Thirty times locked away from reality and the color-ed world that spun along without me. Time seemed to stop when I was shut away from my routine. Days inched along, blending into long bouts of waiting for medicine to take effect. I always came through those times stronger for having made it back out.

The sun was still bright, still lighting up the world, even mine. I thought of the times I had been so desperate that I had tried to take my own life. Pills downed in despair, try-ing to shut out the darkness that pressed in on me. Three times I had been rushed to the hospital to be talked into swallowing charcoal to counteract the pills I had taken. One time, I had taken pills and seen hallucinations. The doctors had tried to convince me that they didn't give me anything with bugs in it to drink, but my cup seemed full of them all swimming around. The walls had bugs on them too, creeping up and around my spot on the hospital bed.

I couldn't think straight, all those bugs crawling about. Faces appeared before me, huge and mottled. Voices whispered to me, but I couldn't make out what they were saying. My eyes were heavy with sleep. I would close them only to open them to more bugs creeping, more faces peering down at me.

I blinked back the memories of those darker times and turned my face to the sunlight. It felt good warming my skin. So many times I had shut away the light and curled up within the badness. Now, here at Alyssum, I was relearning to embrace warmth, the love of life that I still carried. And I was doing it in natural surroundings that were just beginning to blossom with life in the world. I found myself focusing on the moment, breathing in and out.

I wondered if others had found comfort in this retreat place. Here in the mountains, I had thrown out all the bad memories, purged myself of the pain, faced it all. And I was still here, still breathing, still coping. I could accept that bad things happened, I just had to move on. It was time.

Ladybug came in and pushed against my legs. I turned and rolled up and onto my feet. I bent down and rubbed her, watched the dog close its eyes and be in the moment. A good scratch was all that the dog needed. Good point. My stomach rumbled, so I went to the kitchen.

Ladybug followed.

The afternoon passed with a nice lunch and much talking. I didn't know I had so much to say. For so long I had been passive, always trying to make sure everyone else was heard, that I had forgotten my own voice. My writing now became my first conversation with my old self.

I looked out at the flowering fruit trees, a blue jay pecking at the tree buds. I watched him twist and turn, peck, and shake. He brushed off his soreness as he sat perched in the tree. I thought I could ease the soreness from my own past with more words written to the world.

I recalled when I was so sad I couldn't make decisions for myself and was placed in a day program. In my twenties, days spent working at arts and crafts, moving fingers while my mind sat, numbed from all the anguish with medications. Medications that made me drool and bob my head while I sewed on in a plastic molded chair.

I remembered the nurse who held my life in her hands. The nurse told me what to do, told me how to be, told me to listen and do what she said or she would send me to the state hospital in Waterbury. The nurse wanted me to comply, wanted me to sit and occupy my hands with crafts, sit in those hard chairs and let the days go by. Every week I would ask to leave and she would mention the hospital and how I still had to learn to listen to her. It made me anxious.

"You will do what I say or you'll go to Waterbury."

She was also my therapist and I had to check in with during each day. I would comply, heed her, try to enjoy bingo and basket weaving.

Panic would fill me. I would sink into a chair to forget the loss of control I had to endure. Days turned into weeks. I formed myself into the chair, formed my thoughts slowly over the loud berating as the neighbors screamed. Inside, I yelled back at them, shrill inside my head while outside, I painted, sewed, and played daily bingo.

I was doped from the medication, lost in my own thoughts as I sat and crafted with a group of others all doing the same. The quiet motions of each, churning into my mind. A painful rift of desperation would seep into me. I would stand up quickly, then sit back down, for there was nowhere to go.

At certain times there were scheduled breaks from the monotony. I would go stand on the front porch of the old hospital and smoke with the others. I would blow smoke into the air, watch it swirl up and around the house, disappear. I wished I could disappear. I thought of ending my life, ending the pain that I was trapped in. But, I continued to craft between smoke breaks. I painted, I scratched out drawings, I sat in the molded chairs, detached from the rest of the group.

And there were nights away from home. Away from my own family. When the nurse thought I was not safe enough to go home, I would be packed off on a bus and taken to Georgia Shore to a residential treatment home. Whether I really needed to go or not was insignificant.

I relented. I climbed up the steps of the short bus and I was taken to Georgia Shore after a day of arts and crafts. I remembered the small bus bouncing through St. Albans and arriving at the place by the lake.

Another twin bed in a small room. My room was a converted porch turned bedroom. It was small but had a nice view of the lake. I would look out at the water, the calm expanse of water that waved a bit with the wind.

The water called to me, stirred my insides. I looked out at it, so calm it looked like I could fall back into it and it would hold me up, rock me gently as I lay on top. I wished to go sit by the shoreline and watch the waves just lap at my feet. And I would learn to breathe. Again and again.

Simple

Would it be so simple
to float away on a wave?

Kick off into the sunset,
paddle away to an island where
love medicates,
neighbors solidify
into relationships,
feet are
buried in the sand,
with the sun refreshing life,
and I am
surrounded only
by loving voices of my boys.

There were meals with strangers, small talk, and no family with me. After meals, I would walk across the street to the lake. Trees grew up on the sandy shore and I walked between them, pressing my hands on the rough, weathered trunks. I would stand by the edge of the water and stare out at the wetness, wish to dive below its surface and swim away.

I would continue to stare out at the lake. Sometimes, there were sailboats in the water and I would watch them until they were just white dots in the distance. I would touch my feet to the water and feel its coldness, feeling like I was connected to something bigger than me and my pain.

I struggled to remain thinking clearly. The medication made things blurry. With feet in the water, I would imagine falling in and floating away, way out to the white boats. I would stand there, letting the water lap against my ankles, let the boats be points of light to look at, let the world keep right on spinning. And I would learn to breathe. Again and again.

Back in the present moment at Alyssum, I recalled other

group homes. One had been just around the corner from my previous house. I would stay there when the neighbors were too loud, when I just wanted to escape, to end my life. At the time, it had seemed like that was the only decision that made any sense. But the doctor would change medication and I would start to feel calmer and better able to handle all the noise.

One night, I sat in a room with another twin bed, with another small window that looked out to a yard with trees. I stared at the green outside and listened to the neighbors as they poisoned my mind. They were hateful, loud, aggressive. I was tired of fighting through the noise. I wanted it to end but I didn't know how to stop them.

I listened, shaking my head to ward off the attack. I looked at the leaves outside, some lit up by the sun that was setting on the horizon. They seemed to shine like stars blowing on the breeze outside. I lifted my head and caught a fresh breath in my small room. I breathed in and out. I counted slowly and I was okay. I was okay in the small room looking out the small window on a world that seemed so very big. I could see the rooftop of my beautiful blue and white home just houses away. Jim would be settling my two boys for bed.

There were others who abused their power, tried to hurt me in their own little ways. Nurses that told me what to do. Threats to get me to conform. Groups sessions to attend to pass the time, endless time. Don't do this or you'll never get out of this place. Do this for me. And I complied and did what was asked so I could go back to my home, back to my family.

One time, when my middle son was young I placed him in home daycare while I worked. The teacher thought that I hurt him. The teacher asked him what I hit him with. He said, "With butterflies." So, she called DCF and they called my husband to pick my son up.

When I finished my shift working as a home visitor, teaching young mother's how to parent, I went to pick him up. No cell phones then, the teacher told me I could no longer be with my son until I talked with the state at DCF. I went to the state office and was brought into a room. They kept me there for three hours, questioning me.

"We can't prove that you hurt your son but we know you have a mental illness. Tell us that it is just too hard and that you hurt him."

"I love my boys. I would never hurt them or anyone."

"It must be hard to be bipolar. It must be hard to be a mom," they persisted. "Did you just get too tired?"

I complied again. I answered their questions as best as I could. I knew I would never hurt anything or anyone. I knew what pain was and didn't want anyone else to feel that.

After three hours, I said, "My brother is a lawyer. Call him." They stopped questioning me.

"We can't prove that you hurt your son. We know you are mentally ill. So we are going to put you on probation for a year, observe you. Perhaps have unannounced visits."

Anger flared inside me. This wasn't fair. I worried about my son. I wanted him to be okay. He was a toddler, not used to me not picking him up. I left the office. Went home where my boys were.

My husband was angry. He told me that the home care teacher had her neighbors examine every inch of our boy. Now we were told by the state not to take him out of that daycare. He was so frustrated. This happened because on the weekends I was a respite provider for children. During an inspection of my home, I told them that I had a mental illness after being asked. They denied me the ability to care for needy children anymore. One boy would see me as I volunteered at the elementary school where my oldest went and he would talk to me.

"Jodi, I miss your home. When can I come back?"

I would bend down and look in his eyes, and smile at him. I had to tell him that he wasn't able to anymore. I didn't tell him that despite picking him up and seeing his parents using drugs while there to get him, I was the one who wasn't fit because of my illness.

I hadn't used drugs since seventeen and a half, since dating my husband and finding that life could be lived without being oblivious. He helped me live again. I loved him for that even more.

So many injustices because I had a label. It frightened people. People who thought they were better, would tell me what to do. Tell me how to live. Sometimes all I wanted to do was to open my mouth and scream at the stigma.

At a hospital stay, when I was in my late twenties, I went to a craft group. There were always crafts to take the mind off the pain. I made a trivet for my mother, lined up the stars and plastered them just so in the form. As I sat there crafting, another patient got up and started screaming. I froze, watched the therapist stand up and try to calm the person down. The man continued to scream. I watched as he started banging his head. Part of me wanted to stand up and start screaming with him. Wanted to yell, tear something, scream with anger at my fear of authority, my fear of living, my trauma, my sadness. I just sat there placing hearts on a form. Staff came in and escorted the man out. I could hear him calling as he was brought down the hall away from the group. I screamed inside my head with him, again and again.

Another nurse at a different stay at the hospital had told me that I was probably bad and that was why the demons were inside me. Said that I was possessed. The nurse told me that I needed to have an exorcism and that would help me regain control. Jim had advocated for the nurse to no longer be present while I was there. The doctors had agreed and I actually felt some control seep back into my life.

So many days sitting in beds, in chairs, on therapist's couches, waiting for that peace to fill me. So many ebbs and flows like the seasons, washing over me as I tried so hard to come to terms with my emotions.

I had tried Crossroads, a half-day program, to learn how to live in the hard moments. I had tried Seneca, an all-day program, where we sat in leather rocking chairs. We would soothe ourselves with the movement of the chairs while we took apart sentences and rewrote our thoughts into more positive affirmations and beliefs. I had participated, wrote out my pain and confusion.

The neighbors never went away. They seeped into every part of my life, came at unexpected moments and harassed my mind. I couldn't escape their wrath. I still feared them.

Now, I was here at Alyssum. Only there were no more nurses or doctors. There were staff who used peer support to help engage with me. Left me to find the solace I needed in the day. They were there to lift me, to share with me, to let me be. And it felt so good.

The neighbors hadn't come today. It had been a long time since I hadn't heard them every morning. Every afternoon as well. Things were clearer for me.

I thanked Mother Mary, Teresa of Avila, and the Little Flower for helping me reach this moment. This time for letting go. I was glad to be here with the mountains about me, with the sun fading in and out through my days. It was beautiful and sad.

I looked down at Ladybug. The dog wagged her tail and sat beside me, the tail thumping on the floor. I put out my hand and let the dog lick it. Friends.

I missed my best friend, my husband. His tireless work ethic, his ability to never give up on me. Ever. I adored him more for it.

Last, I looked to the trees. The brilliant emergence of green foliage all about me. I walked out to the fire pit and sat to soak it all in. Here on this hilltop was a place to begin a new life without baggage.

I looked out over the farmer's field to where the river kept to its meandering. I let more baggage go. Released it like the smoke trails that wound up from the fire pit. Released it from the currents of my mind, let it follow the river into the fading sunlight.

I thought my time here was close to an end. I was ready to go home. I felt empty in a good way. I felt lighter as I stood and stretched my arms to the sky. I wanted the life with my family. And I was going to go after it, chase it, catch it up in my arms and share myself with them. Me, no longer a girl, just a kind, gentle woman. Maybe that was a small thing to be of service to many, but it was what I wanted. And it was really good.

CHAPTER FOURTEEN

I left the retreat house with my husband and little boy. We drove through the winding mountain top, stopping at a waterfall by the side of the road. We all got out and walked across a wooden bridge where the river was churning below us. I looked up the steep side of the mountain and watched the water fall down to a pool below the bridge. Cool air greeted us while my son raced back and forth on the walkway. I breathed in deeply, inhaling the scent of water and crisp greenery that clung to the hillside. It was a good moment.

We stood there looking out at the water, breathing in the cool mountain air, refreshed to be with each other. Our son stomped on the wooden bridge, smiling to be with us. The bugs were out but they weren't bad. They buzzed about but did not bother us. I leaned toward my husband and kissed him there on the bridge. He kissed me back. We were back together.

Then, we were back in the car unwinding down the hill, back to our town, back to our street, back to our home. When the car pulled in, it was quiet. The three of us walked into the living room and sat in silence. My son curled up on my lap, and we listened to his chatter. I was home.

Months slid by and I fell into a routine so familiar. I worked at the preschool. I brought my son to the Rainbow Room there and went to be with the toddlers in the Sunshine Room. The summer slid by and I found comfort in the lightness of the season. We made mud pies at school, picked mint to suck on, planted flowers and potatoes. The director, Sue brought the outside to life. She had us share the creative healing power of plant life with the children and it helped us too.

Fall came with its sharp snap of coldness. The leaves came down and my son jumped in the piles we raked up. I sat outside with my family, watching the leaves turn from green to orange, then brown and to the ground. The nights were cool but I was okay.

The neighbors still came. Still haunted me during the day, scared me at night. They were a menace that I fought everyday. *Just another voice talking next door*, I tried to tell myself. But their loudness was invasive, seeped into my routine, made me cry into my husband's arms.

My son dressed in various costumes most days before Halloween. He was an astronaut, a fireman, a dragon, and a dinosaur. I loved the way he became what he dressed as. His imagination was wonderful to share. I draped gaudy necklaces about my neck, wrapped scarves around my head, put on sunglasses and gloves. We played in the cool days of Fall.

Winter came fast and with it, the snow. Landscape changed into covered lumps of whiteness. Patio chairs hidden, snow piled against the drive, and the cold biting our faces. But we put up Christmas decorations, got a real tree to put up in the living room, listened to carols. And I was happy for the moment. Happy to be with my family at home. I just wished the neighbors would disappear.

January, 2014 was half-way gone now. I still sat with the neighbors' abuse, still unable to rid myself of the constant harassment that invaded my space. They were loud today, bursting into my thoughts, calling forth cruelty to invade my day. I shook my head to rid the noise, let myself breathe in and out for clarity. I could cope.

For I had been coping since I returned home. Since I

had been back, I was working, caring for my family, and keeping safe. I had thoughts of harm but had managed to push them away, throw them off my shoulders and focus on the present.

I looked out the window at the snow falling. Thick flakes pushed their way down to the ground stuck in piled drifts about the yard. My son would like to stomp in all that snow. He was a kindergartner now. He was at school, where recess would find him with a mitten full of snow, lips cold from tasting, a laugh echoed in the winter air. He was joyful.

I recalled the news from the specialist. How Michael was going to need growth hormone shots if he was to grow. He had cried big crocodile tears on the way home after learning the news. A shot a day until he was eighteen. And the expense of the shots was certainly a factor. It was going to be around five hundred dollars a month for the copay. I didn't know where that money was going to come from.

I bit my lip, bringing myself back to my living room. We had painted it brown with an added green freize, a Greek, key-patterned, strip of wallpaper. It lightened the room up. I looked at the mirror, the plates on the wall, Greek goddesses in cream and burgundy. I looked at the mural of Sappho, the first woman poet. Strength was on my walls. Women with strength.

I would have strength as well. I shook my head, hearing laughter from the neighbors and tried to remain grounded within the room. It was a comfortable space. The couch beneath me was soft, muted green, comfortable. The leather sofa and chair were smooth resting spots. The yellow desk was a reminder that only a few short hours ago, my husband had been home working. The electric piano was a reminder of what my son could become with practice.

I closed my eyes, willed myself energy. I was going to dance tonight. I had begun Jazzercise again and it felt good. I had quit smoking, had fallen back twice, but was certain that I could keep it at bay. I wanted my health. I desperately needed to be well.

I looked down at the sweater that my husband and son had bought me. It sparkled, that's why they had picked it out. The sparkles. I turned back and forth in the light, catching the shimmer of the sequins and glitter. It made me smile.

Soon, it would be group therapy. I needed to get ready for that. Needed to go and face the neighbors with a bit of armor. Perhaps the words that I found today would bring comfort, would aid in my battle.

Group Therapy

We sit in circles
Every encounter,
Staring into the sadness
That sits us there,
Aware that we all share
The poignant pain
Of being misunderstood.
I should speak up,
Scream at the voices,
The neighbors too noisy
In my mind. But I am the kind
That doesn't want a fuss,
Must try to remain calm
Even when the scars
Bust open and I bleed

From the palms of my hands.

Group therapy was made up of seven women sitting in chairs as we expressed our pain. The group leader would talk to us about PTSD and the actual brain chemistry that was affecting each one of them. We would check in to see how each other had overcome hardships during the week. A connection was often made between thoughts and actions. Most were stuck in the paralyzing pain that came with each new day.

I sometimes felt like the room was closing in on me, where I couldn't breathe unless I left. So I sometimes left early, slipped outside and had a cigarette. I still couldn't quit the habit and it was getting in the way of my relationship with my husband. He cared about me, wanted me to be healthy. I didn't know how to let go.

The neighbors laughed at me, called me evil. I cringed at their harsh words, wished I could fade them out, make them leave. They only grew stronger. I was depressed. I couldn't sleep without nightmares, would I ever be okay?

I thought back to the retreat house. Thought of its snow-covered gardens, the hills bare, the cornfields just stalks of what was to come again. The cows in the barn with their breath in smoke. And the river.

The river meandering, endless current beneath ice and cold. The rocks standing guard at the edge of the banks, waiting for others to find just the right flat one. Maybe make a ladybug out of it. Ice formed on its edges. No one would visit its banks now. It would continue to move, swell with thin layers of ice on parts ever in motion.

I wished I could visit. But I couldn't go back yet. Couldn't face the isolation and fear that I might find. I was different from almost a year ago. And still the same. I was a mixture of both in this world. And I realized that maybe that was okay.

I was okay. I was going to make it. I was going to be strong. I was a fighter. I was going to keep on.

I looked back at the snow, soft whiteness now falling straight down. A layer of comfort to hide the dirty slush. It looked peaceful outside. I breathed in. I could feel the peacefulness calm me. I breathed out. Yes, I was a survivor.

CHAPTER FIFTEEN

The snow faded from my view as I froze in a moment of remembering. September 19, 1999. I had been teaching sixth grade. The class was filled with energy. Mornings, I would stand before them and give them a prompt, an opening line to start a poem of their choice. The Sunday before I resumed my class, I was driving in St. Albans, my home then. Jim and I had just bought our first home there when we were 23.

My second son and my client Pat, an adult woman who lived with a disability, sat beside me. Apparently, I was only allowed to care for adults. I was supposed to be caring for her in the evenings, since Pat couldn't care for herself. We stopped to make a left turn.

I looked again in the rear view mirror, the car behind was coming up fast. I couldn't understand why it was still coming so fast. The driver was hanging out the window yelling to someone. Time became confused when his car slammed into mine.

I heard the metal breaking, felt our car pushed into the other lane of oncoming traffic.

My foot felt for the brake, and tried to hit it again and again. My neck hurt from being thrown forward and then back. I couldn't keep my eyes open. My son was crying, Pat was crying, and I was so tired. Blackness.

Man or God's Plan

The men came and one held my head in place,
like the grace of God keeping me still
as the will of my efforts split like the back end

of my car, caging around my toddler safe in his seat.
I felt the defeat of purpose, the ground coming
closer as I nosed down and that man or God's plan
kept me awake, shaking the soil, the turmoil
from my dark eyes and into the bus
that drove us up the hill to help. So quiet
in the afterthought, a p.s. addendum
to an accident where the other car's driver
never understood what his actions should have been
back then.

I opened my eyes. A firefighter was supporting my neck, telling me not to move. I felt stiff all over. I called out my son's name. He didn't answer.

"He's safe. He's in an ambulance. So is Pat. They are okay. Don't move," the firefighter said calmly.

My back hurt. My head was sore. I wanted to curl up and sleep. What had happened?

Then, I was lifted and placed in an ambulance. I could hear my son calling for me. Little six-year old Andy. I tried to answer him back but the door was closing on me. The ambulance carried me to the hospital. All three of us were placed in separate ambulances despite my protests that they should be with me. They drove us all to the hospital.

I watched the fluorescent lights passing above me as I was wheeled down a hall.

X-rays of the top of my back. Nothing seemed broken. I felt bruised. I felt hurt. I was placed in a room for observation. Andrew and Pat were there. They were safe. The driver of the other car was behind the curtain near me.

"I'll pay for everything," I heard him say. He was young, cut up, scared.

I said nothing. I was tired, wanting only to go home

and sleep.

The agency couldn't find someone to come and get Pat so I agreed to keep Pat with me even though I ached all over. My six-year-old sat on my bed, rubbing my leg. I squeezed his hand.

Hours later, I was taken home in a cab with Pat and my son. We curled up on the couch and put the television on for a comforting sound. No one talked much. I felt sore, beaten. My neck hurt. I just wanted to sleep. I cared for Pat and Andrew until their bedtime.

Night swallowed me up in dreams. I felt the crunch of the metal, felt the car pushed into traffic, felt the car push me forward and back. Then sleep came in blackness as I waited for Jim to come home.

Days of stiffness turned my back into one painful ache. It hurt to move. Twisting was an effort. Why did I still hurt?

Months of pain. More doctors. No one understood why I was still in pain. More doctors. Hard to move about. More months. I hired a lawyer to try to help me pay for the doctor bills that were piling up. Physical therapy wasn't helping. I couldn't work.

Things got worse. I could barely walk without my back flaring in pain. I tried pain medication, and a Tenz unit for relief. Massage. I grew depressed with the pain. I could no longer teach.

My mother brought me a wheelchair for long periods when I had to be out. At the supermarket, I used the electric cart to help me shop.

More doctors. The months slipped into years, and I was in so much pain. I could no longer roll about on the floor with my boys. We used to camp every year. No more.

I couldn't do it. My back limited me in what I could do. The insurance wouldn't authorize an MRI, and I was desperate. The doctors ordered more physical therapy.

I went to a program from 9 a.m. to 5 p.m. for five weeks. Intensive therapy, muscle strengthening, adaptive physical therapy, I cried myself to sleep at night. Then went back to try it again and again. Biofeedback was prescribed, group therapy was rigorous. I cried until no more tears would fall. Then, I shook with tearless sadness.

In 2002, I met with Doctor Monssey. He was from the Spine Institute and immediately ordered an MRI. He fought the insurance company, they relented, and I was allowed to have it.

I tried trigger-point injections to release the low back from pain. The shot needles were as long as unsharpened pencils. They didn't work. The numbing agent for the needle insertion was the rare moment of relief that I got from the procedure.

Doctor Monssey had me return to his office. He found the problem in my back. My lower spine was cracked. No amount of physical therapy was going to fix the break. Surgery to fuse the spine was the choice he recommended. Surgery had risks. I had to decide.

It wasn't much of a choice. I couldn't keep living in a wheelchair. I wanted to live without pain. Wanted to climb stairs, bend, run with my growing children without the flare of pain that consumed me as always.

Depression took hold and I was hospitalized again. I worried about making it through the surgery. I worried about being paralyzed. I worried. And with the worry came the neighbors' hateful words. Their whispered threats, their anger at me.

"So easy to die. Just go ahead, let go."

I remembered curling up on a mattress on the floor in a padded room. I rocked myself while the neighbors cursed me. I recalled a doctor coming in and putting a Lorazepam under my tongue to calm me. He was kind, gentle. He tried to comfort me from the harsh noise in my head. I was safe, he would say. He wouldn't let me die. I closed my eyes and pressed back against the noise in my head. Calmness settled inside my thoughts and I grew sleepy. I drifted off in a drugged sense of safety.

Days slid by a foggy mind. I slept often, I walked the halls in a drugged state. I curled up behind the safety of a locked door. Gradually, my mind cleared and I was able to focus on more than just the neighbors and their angry talk. I went to groups. I talked. I was able to rationally consider the surgery option.

I became more aware of my surroundings, noted the other patients, each in their own traumatic stupor. I kept to the groups, showered every morning, and wrote every day. In the chaos of the floor, I learned to be in the moment. When someone went running past my door, ranting, I fought the urge to hide and kept to my writing. I continued to seek out ways to help myself. I talked to the nurses on staff and participated in the scheduled groups.

Then, I was out of the hospital. Away from the nurses, the doctors, and comfortable with my decision to have the surgery. I prepped myself with education and determination to see it through.

Surgery, nearly three years after the accident happened. I wasn't prepared for the after-effects of the surgery. I was in the hospital on morphine for days. I swam to the surface of consciousness only to push the button and let the morphine float me away. One day, I remembered my mother-in-law spooning red jello into my mouth. It tasted so good.

The surgery left me with two long scars on my back and one down my stomach. They had gone into my hip bone and taken pieces to build up my spine where it was cracked. They had gone through my stomach and also my back to fix the spine.

I lived in a brace for several weeks. They brought a bed into the living room downstairs at home where I slept off and on while my wounds healed. A visiting nurse came to check on me.

Eventually, the nurse took out the staples in my stomach that held my incision closed. My oldest son watched as the nurse struggled to get them out. He was curious.

After three years of agonized pain and one year of healing from the surgery I was able to walk into the lawyer's office. The other driver's insurance didn't want to pay the full amount. I read a letter I had written. I wasn't going to get anything for pain and suffering. A third would go to insurance, a third would go to the lawyer, and my third would barely pay for the credit card bills I was left with since the accident. They eventually agreed.

I had reached out my hand to the other driver. That was a hard thing to do. Shake the hand of the man that had brought this pain to my world. My fingers touched his. Anger shook me as I gripped his hand. It didn't stay though; he was just a young driver who did a stupid thing.

And then it was done. I was left with scars, and atrophied muscles in my back that still hurt. But I could run. I could walk. I was alive with less pain. I was a survivor once more.

The physical pain almost matched the mental creations that froze my being, terrorized my thoughts, left me a victim.

But I was more than hurt. I fought each day, each moment to overcome the numbing fear that tried to cast out my own being, make me a ghost, empty, floating without will. I stood to take each step forward, face up, following the brightness, the path that presented life, okay with myself, okay to remain. I battled because it was all I had ever known and some days, I was found in the light and bathed in such happiness that surrounded me in the beauty of living.

I blinked back the memory. The snow was still coming down. I was no longer living in St. Albans. I was in South Burlington. My oldest had his own place. My middle son was grown and trying to figure out his life. I had another son. And he was six. And I had my husband.

I remembered when I quit smoking and prepared my body for another baby. My husband and I cried as we made love. We had been through so much and wanted to love another baby. We began a new chapter in life.

Next month we would celebrate twenty-five years of marriage. That was something. That was something real. He was always there for me. I loved that man so.

I wished the neighbors would move off. I didn't wish them on anyone, that would be cruel. I just wanted them to leave me alone. They were holding me back. I was keeping myself back. How could I rid myself of these terrible conversations?

I had overcome so many hardships. I breathed in and out. I felt the couch beneath me. I looked at my living room. The mirror still had Christmas figures on it. *That should come down*, I thought. It was no longer the holiday season in my church year. Soon it would be Lent.

I picked up my book. The diary of St. Faustina. I prayed for a message from God. A reason why hardships happened. How to keep on when depression pointed at me, laughed at me, made me want to curl up into nothing.

I looked outside. The snow still fell. It placed a blanket of whiteness over the yard. I thought of falling back into it. Maybe making a snow angel in it with my youngest. There was still a lot left to do. I scratched at the nicotine patch taped to my shoulder. Yes, I was not smoking now.

Still wanted to puff out the smoke but knew it was a death sentence. And I wanted to live.

Wanted life to be less complicated. Smoking just complicated things.

In the silence I prayed. I listened to soft music as the snow piled up outside. While dreams stirred in my fingers, I wrote out my pain. Let it drift through the currents of each fingertip until it left me and was placed on the black and white of the page.

I thought of when I was most afraid. It was when I was alone and the neighbors came. I listened to their harsh words, their hateful way of turning thoughts into painful reminders of what I really thought of myself. I needed to learn to love myself like I loved my family. How?

I breathed in. I breathed out. I was learning to use my breath as a tool for coping, grounding. My therapist had practiced it with me. I let my breath calm me, comfort me, to become the present moment that I listened to.

The snow fell outside the window, and I watched it come down, softly cleaning the world with its cover. I looked at the thick flakes wiping the front yard, covering the trees, the ground, the driveway. I was quiet, the neighbors were fading, I was alone without fear.

I still watched the snow come down, wishing my son

was home so we could pile up into winter coats and go out and catch the flakes, make snow angels, play in the whiteness. I wanted to embrace life and live the normal moments that made up days that counted. If only I could hold onto these thoughts, pull them out when things were stressful. Maybe I could.

CHAPTER SIXTEEN

March came and with it I started a new job helping people again. I helped people who happened to live with mental illness to find employment. It was difficult work, but so much quieter than working with toddlers. I liked having an office, going out to businesses, and meeting with clients. A year had passed since I had been at Allysum. I often thought of the farmhouse there. Thought of the walks through the farmer's fields to the river. Tried to visualize the peace I had found there. And I was getting along as best I could.

I looked out at the trees starting to develop leaves, to the grass slowly turning green from the bland. From my spot, I watched a woodpecker with its bright red head pecking at my front tree. Things were getting to be okay.

Months slipped by with work and family, and watching Michael grow. His shots were helping him, already he had grown three inches. And he didn't cry very much when I had to give him the shot.

Outside, it was now summer. There were chipmunks all over the yard. I could spot their holes here and there. I liked to watch as they stuffed their cheeks with nuts until they looked ready to explode and then race to one of their holes. Bumblebees alighted on the small purple flowers, low to the ground, and gathered the nectar. I watched them dive their noses into the middle of a flower, their legs holding tight to the petals.

I sat in a chair out back watching the quietness. The neighbors were still right there beyond the invisible wall. Still trying to tear me down. During the day I could fight them, keep strong but when night came I seemed too tired to ignore them.

With summer here the sun was brighter, and brought its warmth to me. I often found time to sit in the backyard and feel the heat on my face. I continued to work and find pleasure in normalcy with that and my family.

One night, we had a fire out back and sat around its flames roasting marshmallows. The fire's smoke trailed up into the dark sky. I smelled its woody scent, and watched the orange flames surround the logs. It was a normal night.

Campfire

We camped beside the fireplace in our backyard
with the fire licking the cut limbs from the old trees,
my husband bent on his knees feeding the flames
As Michael danced like the flitting lightning bugs
come June.
It was too soon to spoil as we sang like we were
away,
off on a camping adventure yet without the usual rain
that stained our tents, shattered the dreams
of normalcy out in the woods kind of dreaming delight.
I could have stayed
all night beside the two, careless creations
of comments against the stars brightness between
the green leaves of outstretched arms grasping for the
light
up there. I stared into the red and orange movement
so alive in this place,
while the stars and the lightning bugs blinked
above the ground. I found that I was fueled,
fed by the desire for normalcy, for the voices in my

head,
the hurt in my soul that could somehow be avoided
by this night here, this time without fear, with my
dear
sweet boys.

The neighbors came often and I fought their words. I willed myself to keep them beyond the wall, away from me. They were coming more often and it hurt that I couldn't push them aside. Even the sun wasn't helping now. I felt lost as if weights were dragging me down.

One Tuesday evening after a normal day of caring for my son, I stood in the kitchen in front of the cupboard where I kept all my medicine. The neighbors urged me to hurt myself. Just take some pills and be done with it. It was late. Everyone was asleep. I too should have been sleeping, but I couldn't settle, couldn't keep to my breathing.

I walked to my room and looked down at my husband sleeping. I wanted to shake him, make him hold me, tell me this would end. I let him keep right on sleeping as I went back into the kitchen.

I took down the bottle of Lorazepam and held it in my hand. The neighbors urged me on, told me it made sense to give in and find some final peace. I unscrewed the lid and poured them out in the palm of my hand. A handful of tiny white pills that could do so much damage.

"Do it," I heard. "Just do it. You're no good, your family needs you gone. You hurt people too much." Their words seemed louder than just beyond the wall.

I lifted my hand to my mouth. Then, put it back down. No. Yes. No. Yes. I filled a glass with water. Then, I stuffed the pills into my mouth and swallowed them down with the water. I stood in the kitchen for a few minutes. Laughter all about. Such mean laughter. I shook my head to clear my thoughts. What had I just done? Was I ready to die? I leaned against the cupboard.

Maybe I could just sleep it off and no one would know what I had done. I walked to the bedroom and got in bed with my husband. The neighbors hissed at me, told me to sleep, leave Jim alone. I watched him sleep. I really loved him, loved every minute we were together. It was too hard with the neighbors, nights were so bad I couldn't stand it. But I loved my family, loved the quiet times with my husband where we only need be in the same room to be reassured.

He was my life and I had made a promise to be with him. I was getting sleepy, the medicine was taking effect. I reached out a hand and placed it on his shoulder. He turned to me.

"I did something stupid."

He brought me to the hospital and dropped me off in the emergency room. He was angry, frustrated at me, worried about me. The nurses brought me right in. I told them that I had taken about 30 Lorazepams and was sleepy. They told me to stay awake. I was drowsy, tried to fight the effect of the drug, and I fell into a deep sleep.

I woke up with an IV in my arm. They had been giving me solutions to counter the drugs. I was seeing double and when I moved my head the room moved too. My bed seemed to be sliding closer to the door. The person watching over me looked at me and his head seemed as big as a blown up balloon. I swam in and out of consciousness, trying to figure out where I was and why I was there.

When I came to, I sat up in bed and had to use the bathroom. They had a potty chair next to my bed. I couldn't walk on my own, my legs didn't seem to want to work together. The person in my room helped me get to the toilet and back into the bed.

The residents came trying to talk me into being admitted into the hospital. I didn't want to do that. I wanted to go home. They said that wasn't an option. I said I would go to ASSIST.

ASSIST is a six-bed, residential care unit at Burlington's Howard Center that I used when I didn't quite need hospital care. They said that if I went home they would hold me in the hospital for a certain amount of hours. I said I'd go to ASSIST again.

My sister came with her friend Anne Marie, and they visited. Everyone looked like they had double eyes on their faces. I was tired. I couldn't focus on what they were saying. My head was cloudy, thoughts mixed up. I fell asleep again. I woke to laughter in the room. It was the neighbors. The neighbors laughed at me. I wasn't amused. That afternoon my sister and Anne Marie brought me to ASSIST. They left shortly after. And then I was alone in a strange room.

Again.

I sat on another twin bed and waited for my husband to come and visit. I wished I could take it back, go back to the time I was staring down at him while he slept and cling to him instead of the pills. I just couldn't seem to want to live with the neighbors around. They wore me down and I was despairing.

I stood up and walked about ASSIST's great room just outside my door. I sat on a couch. I rocked in a chair. I went outside and walked up and down the gravel path. It was wet outside but I didn't care. The summer day was dark in my head, and I was alone.

Inside, one of the workers tried talking to me. I didn't

want to talk. They tried to get me to say whether I felt safe. I was up and down with my mood, I couldn't decide. I thought things would be better if I was gone.

Jim came to visit and brought me my computer and clothes. He didn't say too much. I knew I had hurt him. I tried to let go of the guilt. I wanted to live with him. I did want to live.

Right? Just not with the neighbors so close.

That night, I curled up in bed and rocked myself to sleep. Jim had brought my CPAP breathing machine so I used that. My head still hurt, I ached inside my chest, I really missed Jim and our own bed.

They had accidentally given insulin to me twice, so every hour they woke me up to check my blood sugar numbers. I tried really hard to get my fingers to move right so I could get the blood to match the strip. I was still confused and so tired. They had to use more than one strip at times.

I had lived with type 1 diabetes since my 20's when a psychiatric medicine hurt my pancreas. I had to adjust to using insulin everyday. One doctor told me that I would have gotten diabetes anyway, when I was in my seventies. It didn't help.

Morning came with brightness. My head still hurt and I was still seeing double faces, especially eyes. I got up and went to shower. A shower always made me feel better. I walked around the grounds outside and smoked.

I had been trying so hard not to smoke but the stress had taken its toll. The neighbors laughed at my foolishness, urged on my bad habits. Would I always be plagued with these demons?

Didn't I try to be good? Didn't I help others? Why was I doing this to myself? And if I was doing it, how could I stop it? I wanted to let them go.

I walked about on the grass, passed a snake and watched it curl up to the building. White rocks lined a gully and I stepped over them and onto another patch of grass. Chairs were lined up by the edge of the ravine and I could look out into the trees and watch the small animals.

Soft Blades

I am in the soft blades back of ASSIST
where they insist that I stay here,
the fear that I will hurt, desert my own being
into fleeing from this world. I hold onto the last
moment of sanity when I was back in Rochester
by the river below Alyssum. Where the flowers
came up to the sides, that parted the way
down to the rocks on the shore, more running
current to pass my hands through, feel the cold
ice sensation of the seconds, release
the stuffed, stifled pain in my chest,
blow out the stale breath from the rest
and learn to be.
Now I lean on a folding chair, creaking its
limitations of my burden, the small
den of foxes down the ravine between
this building and my old workplace.
I search out the branches loaded with summer's
bounty, life alive in the verdant scenery.
The greenery stirs my insides, makes my face
flush, blush to thoughts of young love
with my love so far from me right now.
Somehow I want to climb out of this hole,
this temporary setback in a chair
that wobbles, and roam my way

back to him, to home, to my family.
I am in the soft blades back of ASSIST
and I insist to stay here on Earth,
To live, to give, to be just Jodi.

Squirrels were all about, wriggling their tails, climbing
trees. I was reminded of the retreat house, Alyssum, where
I would sit in the back and watch the creatures there. Nature could be found anywhere. Was that feeling, that passion, that life-giving breath of fresh air inside me wherever
I was? Could I find it and relieve the pain that still irritated
me, still stuck to me? I breathed in deeply and let it out.
Again, I focused on my breath. In and out I breathed, as
I watched the birds and the squirrels wander about their
home.

I could be here in my own body without fear. The
neighbors called, whispered my name. I breathed in. I
breathed out. The neighbors threatened, said I deserved to
die. I breathed in. I breathed out through the loudness in
my mind.

"I don't have to fear you," I said towards the trees. "I
am safe. I am here. I am here."

I rocked in the chair, breathing in, breathing out. Again
and again I breathed as I observed the ravine. I looked at
the trees, their trunks springing up from the bottom like
arms reaching out to the sky. I noticed the green leaves
tangled in each other's way. It was hard to tell where one
treetop began apart from the others. I thought there must
be birds up in the leaves, sitting on branches, listening. I
searched the leaves but there were too many, and I couldn't
see between them.

Then, I stared up at the sky and watched the thin
clouds move above in the pale blueness. I was alive. I was

safe. I was going to do what was best for myself. I stood up and walked to the edge of the ravine. Peering way down, I could see the thin water trail that wound about the trees. I heard crows squawking from a branch, and felt the first drops of a rain shower.

I was here, breathing and maybe that was okay for now. I wasn't sure. I thought back to times like this when I was in a program or at a hospital. The view could change but nature was alive. I liked the way the trees seemed like tall giants, the ravine a hole they grew out of. Could I crawl out of the dark hole I was in? I turned and made my way back over the white rocks and onto the path that led inside.

The doctor was waiting for me, so I went with him to a room. We sat in chairs across from each other with the resident doctor sitting at his side. The leading doctor had black, wire-rimmed spectacles perched on the tip of his nose, wavy hair brushed back, a serious expression on his face. The resident had blond hair down to her shoulders, and an earnest look on her face. They were concerned for my safety. They were concerned that I might try to hurt myself. They wanted me to be voluntarily admitted into the hospital.

I didn't want to go. I wanted to go home and pretend I hadn't tried to kill myself. Pretend that I didn't hear the neighbors' commanding voices. Pretend that I was all right. I told them I didn't want to go.

The doctor said that they would involuntarily commit me if I refused to go on my own. I was mad, frustrated, and scared. The neighbors laughed. I had no choice. I was going to the hospital. The hospital had no green grass to sit amidst. No ravine with trees to shelter me. No squirrels and no crows.

A case worker came in and talked to me. She was an older woman with gray hair down to her shoulders, glasses on her face. She looked like an ex-smoker with telltale lines on her face. Her name was Joan.

"It's best if you voluntarily go into the hospital," she said.

"I don't want to go. I just want it to be all over," I said quietly.

Joan studied me and put on a thin smile.

"Maybe they can help you at the hospital. They can keep you safe for awhile. It's better to not involve the police. If the police get involved, you could end up in Rutland," she said and then paused. She spoke softly, "You don't want to go down there."

I looked helplessly at Joan but found little comfort. I turned and looked out at the yard. An apartment building stood just beyond the trees. Short trees and a fence blocked some of the view. I watched the orange lilies sway. I rocked myself in the chair.

"I don't have a choice," I said, resigning to going back to the hospital. It would now be more than thirty times there. I didn't want to think of the toll it would take on my family's finances.

Money was already tight. I just wanted it all to be over.

"No, there really is no choice right now but to go," Joan said quietly. "You might find some relief from your troubles. You'll be safe too."

I could barely acknowledge Joan. I wanted to stand and race from the room, hide from the neighbors' upsetting words. I needed a thicker wall to protect myself. Instead I stood up and nodded in agreement.

"Okay, I'll go," I said, almost to myself. Joan nodded and stood up too. Our meeting was over, so I left and went to my room to collect my things.

I left ASSIST with Michelle, a young girl just out of school. She drove me to the hospital in a standard car. As Michelle shifted, she spoke about everyday events, the weather. I listened to the young girl talk.

"Can I smoke in here?" I asked Michelle.

"Sure. I'm a closet smoker myself." She looked at me.

"Would you like one?" I asked Michelle.

"I shouldn't, but okay."

Michelle drove while we each smoked a cigarette. We drove in silence with smoke trailing out the windows. It was a different experience to smoke in a car. I didn't do that with my family. I blew the smoke out the window watching it disappear beyond the car. I breathed in. I breathed out. I could handle this. I would be okay. I hoped I had a view at the hospital.

CHAPTER SEVENTEEN

Shepherdson Three was the name of the floor. The door was locked, since this wasn't supposed to be an acute care floor. I'd been on the acute floor several times.

Really chaotic up there. No, I was here. I had to accept that. No padded room on this floor.

I screamed in my head, but was polite throughout the paperwork and the intake procedure.

A resident brought me to my room. Another twin bed with a sheet and blanket. There was a low, whining noise that irritated me but I said nothing. The bathroom adjoining the room was mine. So, I wouldn't be sharing it with anyone. I looked out the window at the metal vents and machinery on the roof next to my window. I could see other windows on the side of the building adjacent to mine. One window had a get-well-soon balloon. I couldn't see the patient, just the yellow balloon in the window. I hoped he or she was doing better than I felt.

When I was finished with the intake and they had searched me for prohibited items, taking my lighter away from me, I walked the loop around the floor. Open doors revealed other patients sitting or lying on their beds. Some were in hospital scrubs, some in pajamas, some in regular clothes. Nothing with drawstrings though. They had taken my shorts with the string so I wouldn't wrap it around my neck.

I looked into the dining room. The flat-screen TV was flickering in a dark room. Rows of empty tables and chairs filled the hall. Nothing looked comfortable. I went back to my room.

I tried to think of what to do. I wasn't tired, but I curled up anyway. I lay on the bed and looked out the window at the industrialized sight. No grass or sunshine to distract me. A whining noise that irked me. I counted in my head to remain calm.

Anxiety came. I was behind a locked door and had no choice but to accept it. I wanted to run down the hall, fling myself at the door, and race away. Far away, where the neighbors couldn't find me. That was wishful thinking. I had to face them soon. Had to come to terms with the noise. Had to find ways to be peaceful.

The Metal Box

I am caged behind the metal box
out my window. The whirling blades
of fan belts and machinery
that keeps this place running.
I have no vista, no place to set my sights
and explore the natural world.
The walls in my room are mute yellow,
Sick vomit paint that upsets my soul.
There are no pictures to climb into,
no bolted down screens through which to feel
the whiff of a breath from the lake below.
I look between the gray steel parts,
And the locked window, to a bleak sky
where parts of me train on the blueness,
the color of a child's balloon at a fair,
a happy smile after a cry, the eyes
Of my mother and me, the joy
of Jim seeing to me from behind
the mask of sadness and the pained
voices that startle into my madness.

I bless that there is at least
that blue, that impossible lifting
of white clouds that skip over the color
like rocks on water, passing over
as waves on the water. I sit
on the edge of my twin bed, again,
my elephant blanket my sister bought,
my security, as I cradle myself
in my own arms and rock
to the gentle blue movement beyond the steel.

A nurse poked her head in the room.
"Just checking on you," she said and then left.

A uniformed worker pushed a tray filled with dinner down the hall. I heard the squeak of the wheels, smelled the food. I was hungry. I went to the dining room and found my tray.

Dinner came on trays with green covered plates. Plastic silverware, plastic cups, plastic bowls. I lifted the cover and ate some pasta and sweet potatoes. I saved my apple for later, and the Rice Krispie treat I put aside for my son's visit.

I still didn't know what to do. I was lost with the neighbors commanding me to hurt myself and I felt so unsure of my own actions and abilities to fight them. I went to my room and looked at the green and white walls, the one picture in the room. A picture of flowers bolted to the wall so I wouldn't get an urge to pull it off and smash it somewhere or on someone.

I curled up on my bed with the green blanket and the tiny pillow. I tried to get comfortable, tried to imagine myself being well. Just some hissing, and some curses, and confusion filling up my head. I dozed.

That night, my husband visited with my youngest son. They came and I held my six-year old and hugged him tight to my chest. He cried and we all had a family hug. I wanted to be well so I could go home and care for them. I wanted to go home and be free of the neighbors that wanted me to hurt myself. If I could only let them drift away and not listen to them, maybe their power would go away.

Tomorrow was my youngest son's birthday and I would not be able to be part of his day. He wasn't even supposed to come up onto the floor. There was a no-child policy, but the night nurse had let him in. Tomorrow, he would turn 7 and he would have a party at Pizza Putt, go watch his cousin Nora ride a horse, and then go out to China Buffet. And I would be here, locked up on this floor with the neighbors' voices surrounding me and no smoking to relax me.

My husband and son left and I was alone again. Dark thoughts spiraled in my head. I felt sick. I was fearful. The nurse came in and got my CPAP ready for bed. Another nurse had to sit at my door and watch me sleep with the machine in case I decided to wrap the cord around my neck. I didn't want to do that. But they wouldn't listen, so I stayed silent.

I woke up often to roll onto my side, onto my back, onto my stomach. I fluffed up the tiny pillow and used my arm as a base to cradle it. I was hot. There was a droning noise in my room that was irritating me and I wanted to be home. Morning came slowly.

I got ready in the bathroom, had breakfast, medicine, and insulin, then went back to my room. I didn't know how to act, what to do when all my body wanted was to run away. Go outside and smoke, and smoke, and leave this awful building.

My mother showed up with a loving card. She brought nuts and a deck of playing cards. We played rummy and thirty-one and it helped keep me in the moment. I focused on the cards and not the neighbors. They were grumpy and cruel to me. They're on the other side of the wall, just neighbors fighting, I told myself.

I thought about my son at Pizza Putt and the fun he must be having. I ached to be with him but I was not well enough for a pass. Later that afternoon, my husband came by and we played cards. My father and his wife, Sue stopped by. We all talked. I was open about my condition. I told them I just wanted the neighbors to go away. I was tired of them and needed help. Sue brought a *People* magazine to pass some time. I was getting through time slowly. But I was doing it.

Sunday came. I went to groups on the floor. I watched as others formed in circles around tables and spoke of their pain. One woman's husband had just committed suicide. She shot herself because of the hurt. I sat in flannel pajama pants and a shirt. Another woman with creases around her eyes was mourning over her husband leaving her. Men talked of pain and worries, and some of nothing at all. Many simply stared at the table or the art they manipulated with their hands as they talked. I was silent and observed.

Another group had me make a word collage on white paper. I flipped through magazines as old as 1987, the first year I had been hospitalized. Back then, I could smoke in my room. I had a roommate who was anorexic. I thought back to how different things were then. I wished I could turn back time. But that was before I had a family.

Could I unwind my pain at a cost to my children? Who knew if I would be any better? I had to decide. I was clinging to the comfort found in my husband and children. They were what kept me going despite the struggle.

I left the group and went to my room. I put the collage of words against the wall near the heater. I looked at what I had glued to the page. Control impulses, manage emotions, pictures of crisp orange leaves on a mountainside, a couple holding hands.

Erased

Feelings erased like chalkboards, nothing made much sense.
Words written in whiteness smeared into a mess.
Did I wipe it much too swiftly? Did it fade away this day?
Did someone come to call and I left my thoughts to stray?
Did I let them just take over 'til I had no more for fear?
Like the weed entangled grass, did they come too close and near?
Did they pave the cities passed with the blades of gray cement?
Did they roll away like thunder, will I ever know what's meant?
Who has the sense to answer me while frantic in my mind?
Oh when will I feel whole again and feel life's love defined?
Where is the chalk to write for me, to free me from this board?
Erased but stuck with streaky tears upon this place I'm stored.

A knock at my door and I turned to see Father Pat, my parish priest. I was glad to see him. He came in quietly. I sat with him. We prayed together and I felt moved.

My prayerful life stirred me. I asked for healing. We spoke for a time about my illness. He didn't know I was sick, on disability. I told him of my struggle and he listened quietly. I was open and honest about my condition and he prayed for me, anointed me, gave me reconciliation.

He left saying he would be back. I hugged myself and rocked on my bed. I wished I could see some color. This place was so faded-looking. I closed my eyes and thought back to the retreat house, Alyssum where the river kept up its movement. I could move too. I could move beyond the pain I was stuck in, and had lived in for so long.

I thought to when I stood by the river tossing rocks into the water, releasing stored up memories. I felt small next to the river which moved endlessly and didn't stop for the rocks I threw into its wetness. I wished I could be back there, wanted to go back, and write, and talk, and breathe.

Perhaps, I could do that here without seeing the Green Mountains, without the hillside covered in corn stalks, the cows, the river. I could envision a peaceful place and make it my own. I got my laptop from the nurse's station. I couldn't have the cord of course, but I had battery power for two hours. I sat down on my bed and wrote.

Later, Jim came and visited. He brought me some clothes since I didn't have much from before. He brought me shirts and underclothes. We shared a crossword and said so much with our eyes. I missed him. He missed me. I wanted to go home. He wanted me back home too.

When my husband had gone, I looked through the *People* magazine. Curled up and rested, I tried to distract myself from the neighbors' commands. They wanted to hurt me. Did that mean I wanted to hurt myself? Were they really my own thoughts? I knew somewhere deep inside me I wanted to recover, wanted to be well. I was confused in thought.

Later that night, my oldest son came to visit and brought me a Diet Coke. I sipped the drink while he told me about his latest theories on *Game of Thrones*. I liked listening to him talk. He rubbed my feet while we visited. He brought me cigarettes, but I wasn't allowed outside on a pass until the doctor wrote one. So I imagined smoking in the bathroom, but there were smoke detectors everywhere.

That night, another nurse sat outside my door carefully watching me and my CPAP cord. He had a computer that he probably surfed on between checking on me. I tried to fall asleep quickly, but I was uncomfortable. I turned away from the nurse at my door. It felt weird to have someone watching me sleep and I tried to breathe normally.

Monday began by waking from nightmares so vivid that I felt as if I hadn't slept. I showered, changed clothes, and then curled back up on my bed. The nurse came in and took my CPAP machine. They had watched me through the night to make sure I didn't use it to hurt myself. I was past caring about that. I watched her take it away and waited for the breakfast tray, an omelet which I salted and enjoyed. It felt good to taste food. I lingered over each bite of toast and egg together. I was feeling better. Today, I would see a team of doctors and figure out what strategies would help diminish the neighbors.

A doctor came in and we talked for fifteen minutes. He brought residents with him and they all asked questions. The doctor decided to discontinue prescribing the antidepressant, Wellbutrin since I had started it just two weeks ago. It was the most recent change to my medication but one of its side-effects was suicidal ideation. He also increased my antipsychotic meds.

Morning passed with another visit from Father Pat and groups to fill in the hours. I colored a picture, bright hued lines in a design. It would bring color to my room. Then I walked the halls. I was tired of the blandness, the lack of décor, and drab walls. I walked the loop around the floor again and tried to focus on breathing.

A man walked the loop near me, off in his head somewhere. He looked through people, his eyes seeing something else. I wondered if he would come out of his trance. He continued around the floor always with a nurse assisting him.

I stopped at the nurse's station and looked in. Nurses talked together, some using computers. A nurse looked at me and came to the door.

"Need something?" She leaned against the door and waited for me to reply.

"No, I'm just waiting for my husband," I said.

She went back in the office and closed the door. I turned and walked down the hall and passed a patient in a green, flannel robe, her hair disheveled, a faraway look in her eyes.

I wondered if I too had that look. I went back to my room.

The vents and metal machinery on the roof outside the window glinted in the sun. The brightness came into my room. I thought of stars, a flash of lightning, a burst of sunlight. I lay on the bed and felt the warmth of the light reach me. I breathed in. I breathed out. I ignored the buzzing in my ears. It usually meant the neighbors were coming.

The doctor allowed me to have a two-hour pass to go out with my husband. It couldn't have come soon enough. I tried to focus on breathing, clearing my mind of worries. I sat up in bed and then went to the bathroom. I stared hard at myself in the mirror. It wasn't real glass, hard to see myself in the blurred image that looked back. My blond hair was pulled back in barrettes. My blue eyes looked sad. I tried a smile but it felt tight, fake. I pursed my lips and fluffed my hair. Satisfied I looked presentable, I went by the locked door to wait for my husband.

I saw him as he turned the corner down the hall and came to the locked door. He was buzzed in and I hugged him. He hugged me. We held hands and were buzzed off the floor.

It felt strange to be out in the public hallways with others around me. No locked door.

We passed employees and visitors in the hall. I clung to my husband's hand. The neighbors were hissing at me and I couldn't stand their noise so I squeezed Jim's hand tighter as we walked.

The art on the walls was down and new paintings were being prepared to be hung. Vermont scenes scattered the walls while shapes and lined drawings littered the floor waiting to replace the other art.

Outside the main doors and into the sun, we made our way. We walked the sidewalk to my eldest son's house, holding hands. The sun felt warm on my face and I tilted my head up to capture its warmth. Cars passed and I noted the bright colors in the metal. Pines bordered the parking lot, a dark green against blue sky and white clouds.

Down a grassy field to our oldest son's house. We walked slowly. The grass had just been cut. Its fresh scent greeted me. I breathed deeply. It still smelled like summer, like childhood when I followed behind my father as he mowed trails in the yard for us kids to run in. I remembered my younger brother and I rolling down a hill in the back yard, the cut grass catching in our hair. We didn't care.

I was glad to be outside. My son came out and we visited with him for a bit. I smoked a cigarette and somehow it tasted terrible. My husband had parked the car at our son's and we all walked over to it. I could see the sun, feel its warmth. I raised my head and savored the heat, drops of sweat rolling down my cheeks. I didn't care. It felt good to be in the moment. We got in the car and went home to collect Michael and Andy.

We rolled down the windows and let the fresh air hit us in windy delight. I put my hand out the window and felt the rush of wind on it. We drove down the hill to South Burlington. Michael was all smiles when we arrived. Andy grinned at me and we piled into the small car. We drove to Al's French Fries and had lunch. It was so normal to be sitting in a booth with my family, talking idly about the day, listening to Michael talk about his summer days at camp. It was relaxing, felt real.

After lunch we watched Michael on the playground. He spoke with ease to the other mothers and children there and was all smiles. He was happy. I wanted to be that happy. It really could be an easy thing if only I could decrease my anxiety. The neighbors might lessen their tirade if I could get a handle on the stress.

The visit was too short. Soon, my husband was dropping me off at the doorway to the floor. A nurse buzzed me in. I watched my husband walk away down the hall. I was back. A nurse on duty patted me down, searched my pockets, and checked my shoes for prohibited items. She took the lighter away and said I was clean.

"How are you feeling?" she said staring into my eyes.

She looked sincere. It was Sue, the same nurse I had seen many times before when I was hospitalized. She looked concerned. I lifted my head and looked back.

"Well, I'm back here," I said at last, "so things aren't so great."

"I know," she said. "Try to find some things to occupy your time." She patted my shoulder and left with the lighter. I watched the red-headed nurse walk out of my room and back to the office.

I walked down the white halls, faded color back in view. I sighed and went to the dining room. Some patients were watching *Shark Week* on television. I walked through the dining area to the kitchen and filled a glass with ice and water.

Dinner trays arrived and I sat and ate. A nurse came by and asked if I would like to go out to the garden. I wanted off the floor so I put my name on the list and waited for a security guard to escort me out.

The security guard came to our floor with other patients from the sixth floor. We all walked to the end of the hall to a locked door. Some patients were staring glassy-eyed down the hall. One mumbled to himself while another grinned. I followed behind, wanting to feel the fresh air again. The guard opened the door. We went down a metal stairway to the ground floor. Another guard opened the outside door and we were escorted into a walled garden.

Fresh air filled my lungs and I breathed in deeply. Patients spread out in the open courtyard. Flowers and vegetables lined the walls on all sides bringing much needed color. I looked at the oranges, and reds, and blues of flowers. I looked at the green grass, the marble tables and stools scattered about the yard. I walked over to a table.

The garden was walled in and there was no chance of escape, even if I had wanted to. So I sat on a marble stone, my hands resting on a marble table, and watched the group. A man in a long robe and pants paced back and forth. Another man, dark and young, walked along the wall. Nurses sat on marble stones and chatted. I looked at the brightly-colored flowers and thought of poems in my head, watched as another patient picked a strawberry and ate it. It was a bright, red sweetness that I hadn't seen in a while.

The man in the robe whipped his long hair back from his face and raced around the small garden. The nurses stood up and tried to talk to him, tried to get him to slow down. A young girl with dark hair laughed, her teeth so white against her skin and hair. She was dressed in a t-shirt and shorts, and a robe as well.

I sat on a stone and watched the other patients. A young man leaned against the brick wall staring at the ground. The nurses were back, sitting off to one side. They were young girls, nurses with tattoos on their ankles.

"I'm going to get another tattoo on my day off," said the nurse with the braid. "I want to get it on my neck, but I'm scared."

"You should totally do that," the other nurse with short hair said.

"I don't know," the first one sighed. "I hear it's going to rain on my day off. It might as well rain while I have to work here."

I turned my attention back to the man with the long robe. He was laughing as he touched the vegetables that grew on one side, a green pepper and tomatoes by his hand. He muttered and laughed again. I wondered if it was the sharp color that attracted him to the vegetables. They looked fresh and ripe, vivid greens and reds.

The neighbors showed up within earshot. They circled around me, made me look down at the ground, frozen. I didn't move. I felt that given a chance, I would run. I would run, and run until I could no longer move. Then I would run some more. My body showed none of the anxiety as I crouched on the stone. Fear kept me rooted to the spot. I didn't want the nurses to know I was hearing the neighbors.

Twenty minutes later, the security guard came and opened the door letting us back in and up the stairs to the muted colors of the floor. I went to my room and waited for my night medicine. Then it was time to attempt to dream of better things with the downing of pills and insulin administered. They felt I was safer, so they didn't have a guard at my door while I used my CPAP. There were standard fifteen-minute checks.

I listened to music to drone out the low, whistling sound in my room. That sound was enough to make me crazy. I tried to fluff the tiny pillow, bent it in two, tucked an arm under it, and curled up. I prayed for healing, for my family's safety, for a peaceful sleep.

A nurse poked his head in the room and observed me, just doing bed checks. The nurse left and I closed my eyes. Anxiety crept into my thoughts, I tossed back and forth, willing myself to be calm. I fell into a fitful sleep, opening my eyes every once in awhile as the nurses did regular bed checks.

Morning came and with it, my determination to leave. The social worker said that I was out of network, so it was expensive to keep me in the hospital. They weren't so concerned with my safety, but with how I was going to be able to afford her care. I told them all how much safer I felt, how I was more in control.

The doctors took notes. The social worker took notes. The nurses noted my appearance and eye contact. I was much calmer. I was much improved, if only the neighbors weren't so loud. Staff didn't need to know that though.

I had breakfast and waited for my husband to come up. I agreed to be interviewed by a doctor who was teaching residents. I read my book. I did a crossword. I did a fill-in, and I sat on the edge of the bed. I waited, painfully aware of the noise in my head. I kept distracting myself and the noise of the neighbors decreased to a buzzing in my ears.

I could fight this if I didn't get too tired. When I was tired, the pain came to the surface and I couldn't fight back the nasty remarks. I wished I could take a Lorazepam. But I didn't want staff to know I was feeling weak. So I rocked on the bed, walked a lap around the floor, and waited for Jim.

I was going to be all right. I was a fighter. I could handle this. I could really handle this. I went to my room and flopped on the bed. I turned music on to drown out the whining, whistling noise. I closed my eyes and began to pray.

CHAPTER EIGHTEEN

My husband came and waited with me after I had seen the doctor. The social worker had come in to tell me again that I didn't have in-network insurance coverage and it was expensive to be there. She was being nice, but telling me that I couldn't afford to stay anymore without saying it outright. I told the social worker that I felt safe to go back to ASSIST for a couple days, so it was arranged.

Lunch came and I ate while my husband sat with me. He wouldn't eat any of my plate even though I offered him some. We played gin rummy and did a crossword together. Hours trickled by slowly as we waited for the okay for me to leave.

I signed some paperwork then my husband and I were heading down and out of the building. I passed the newly hung art in the hall, a $1500 painting of geometric shapes. I kept walking.

The air outside felt fresher. I was renewed and hopeful. I wished he was taking me home and not to ASSIST, but maybe tomorrow. For now, I was one step closer to getting home.

I had heard that Robin Williams had taken his own life. I was sad about that and also knew how pain could get in the way of living. Just days ago, I had swallowed a dangerous amount of sedatives and was now trying to get back to some sort of normalcy. People were scared about the attempt. I was scared too.

ASSIST was quiet when I arrived back at the one-story building. Inside, an office with windows was on the right side, and a great room with couches to the left. A flat-screen TV hung on the wall. It was only permitted to be turned on early in the morning or after dinner. A kitchen with a long table was behind a half-wall and there were six bedrooms around the great room. At the far end, was an employees-only door. I went in the office and through another admission process. Questions and then a search of my things, and finally I was free to go outside with my husband. We walked to the backyard and sat at a picnic table under a shelter. Jim had his snacks while I smoked a cigarette.

Normalcy crept back into my life. The yard was covered with flowers in pink, white, and yellow, while butterflies flitted about and landed on cockleburs. It was misty but it was real color, real air. Real. I was out of a locked ward and taking steps toward a real life.

The neighbors were still with me. They hissed and tried to command me. I felt stronger and more in control. I ignored them and talked with Jim. Would this always be my life? Would there a time when I could make the neighbors disappear for good? I didn't know, but I was going to try.

I was getting anxious when we went back inside. Soon my husband would be leaving and I would be alone with strangers. There was one other client at ASSIST and the rest were workers that supervised the night shift.

"I want you home," my husband said to me softly.

I closed my eyes, and wanted it too.

"Maybe they'll let me come home tomorrow," I said.

We held hands in the backyard of ASSIST, watching the flowers, watching the trees sway, watching each other. We didn't need to speak, we were comfortable with one another. We had been through this before.

I Want You Home

"I want you home" were his words I heard
from deep within the well of sadness.
I looked out from so far down inside
and tried to heal, tried to climb my way
out of the dark. He was my spark,
the gift of light that lit the day,
gave me power to stay and continue.
I knew he needed me too.
We stood outside of ASSIST,
the night air thick and hard to breathe,
relief only in the touching of our hands
tight against each other. Another
night we would be apart. My heart
hurt, I cried with him in the night
lit by a pale moon. Soon he would
leave and I had to believe he would
come back for me, healed, safe
back in my fight. Tonight he
wrapped his strength around
both of us, and held us up.
I prayed to our God, I fought
the burden of myself
and chose to keep on.
Dawn would come, and even if
I was numb to the wanting,
I did need my family, my man,
my love to stand with me
through this burning pain.
They were the rain that soaked

Into my charred ruins and brought
me back from the flames.

He left and I went to my room and watched *Vampire
Diaries* until the smell of dinner made me get up and check
to see what was cooking. I helped set the table with the
other client.

We both made a plate of stir-fry over rice. The worker
made a plate. A phone call, and he excused himself from
the table. Then, it was just the two of us with another
staff member. We talked about the sports we used to play
in school. I spoke of my trip to Saratoga. The staffer was
from the Albany area and knew it well.

The other client walked around the great room after
supper. He looked like he didn't know where he was or
why he was here. I tried to steer clear of him, but we both
ended up on opposite-facing couches. He looked at me. I
looked back at him. He was thin, dressed in shorts and a
sweatshirt. He looked lost.

"Is this place safe?" he looked directly at me, questioning.

I nodded yes..

"Are they going to hurt us?" his eyes searching franti-
cally. "Are you going to hurt me?"

Was that how I looked when I was listening to the
neighbors?

"No, you're safe here," I said standing up and walking
to my bedroom.

It was hard to watch others struggle. I felt that I was in
a better place emotionally than I had been. I sat down with
my computer and began tapping on the keys. Soon, I was
lost in my words as evening approached.

I stretched my legs and walked about my small room.

Outside the window, it was turning dark and the outlines of trees were silhouetted in my view. Tall maples, some oaks, and a few scrub trees lined the ravine. I looked toward the sky but it was too dark and cloudy to see any stars. I turned back to my room.

I noted the twin bed with the wrinkled blanket, the metal shelves, a wicker chair with a green cushion. It was a soothing room, the walls a soft color. I knew it was a safe place, but I wanted to be home. Could I go home tomorrow?

An Old Soul

Hello to the old soul sitting with me,
Gasping for another chance
To dance with me,
To hold my hand,
To shake, wake, make me stir.
Help me understand
That life is goodness
Wrapped in our love of others and ourselves.
I left myself alone yesterday,
Forgot the brightness
That can shatter the dark,
A spark in the blackness that can replace the bleak panes
Of distorted glass.
Wipe clear the fog.
I am back inside
Comforting the middle-aged woman
That wants to believe in more
Than the pain, the rain, the stain of past sins.
I rock her, soothe her mistakes, take her in my arms

and hold, fold, mold her into a love that fills me.
This morning there are no stars,
No pinpoints of light outside.
But I sense a glimmer
That breaks, takes, shakes me
Into believing
That I am good enough,
That I can be more than my symptom's chaos,
More than the loss, more than the cost of sadness.
I listen to music that tells me I belong, that I long for
a song of hope.
I turn to my other side,
The one with the gift of sight
That might just delight
In the transformation of my soul completely whole.
The one that time stole before
And now I have back.

    I sank into the wicker chair and closed my eyes. So many times I had lost control over my life. So many times I had been at the mercy of others. There had been good nurses, good doctors that supervised my care, but there had also been negligent ones that only seemed to want the power to control. I shuddered at the thought. Now, I was here and the young doctor was the one that could tell me if I could leave or not. I wouldn't give him any reason to keep me here.

    There really was no place safe from my mind.

    A group session was held later that night. We wrote down things that we enjoyed when we were well, things we would like to do again, and then we scheduled time to fit them into our routine. It was a good exercise, a plan for future days. Thoughts of my family frequently came up when I tried to remember what it was like when I was well. I cared for them and enjoyed time spent with each one of them. I wanted to go back to that, but the neighbors continued to hold me back.

I heard buzzing in my ears, felt fear tickling at the back of my neck, and heard their words attack me. I stood my ground. I breathed in. I breathed out. I walked about the great room and observed, grounding myself within the room. There was lots of artwork from previous clients. Snapshots of mindfulness, moments of clarity and color, bright-hued flowers of hope. I looked them all over. Quotes from others crept up one of the walls. I wanted to write again, but I had to wait by the door for my husband dropping off more insulin.

I was tired and ready for bed. I went to my room and just rested on my bed. As I was lying down, I heard my husband's voice and ran out to meet him. I caught him as he was heading back outside. I walked him to the car where my youngest son was in the backseat. Michael held his hands out to me and I jumped in the car to hold him. Tears came to his soft, young cheeks. I told him I would be home in a couple of days. I just needed a little more time. He cried and I stroked his hair.

I got out of the car and held onto my husband. My son was still tearful so I got back in the car to hold him.

"It's okay to be sad. You're allowed," I said. One more hug and then I was out, standing by Jim.

"We need you home," he whispered in my ear.

I clung to him for a moment then stepped back as he prepared to leave. Another night without my best friend to lie beside. Maybe it would only be one more night. I watched them back out and head home, straining to watch the car's lights as they went down the road and out of sight.

I went inside and sat on a couch. I was lonely and wished I could be in the car with my family, heading home. I thought I was better, the neighbors were not so intense. Was it the medicine working to calm me down? I wasn't sure what was helping, but I felt a bit better. I was still scared for my safety, but I wasn't willing to share that with anyone. That would hold me back from returning to my life.

I went to my room and closed the blinds against the darkness. I looked over at the metal shelves where my few possessions were stashed. My collage caught my eye. I looked at the colorful picture, more color at ASSIST than I had had at the hospital. More to look at.

I sat down on the edge of my bed, on a twin again, narrow and unfamiliar. I wished that tomorrow I could be sleeping in my own bed. Maybe I would be able to leave. I closed my eyes and put on my CPAP. Perhaps the night terrors would diminish and I would have a peaceful sleep. I could only hope.

Night terrors got in the way of my rest. I dreamed of my husband and of running, running after my family. I couldn't catch them in my sleep. I was tired when I arose, but thoughts of going home pushed aside the weariness.

I had gotten an appointment to see Max, my therapist on Monday. I hadn't seen him in almost a year. I missed our regular sessions, but was nervous to be getting back into therapy with him. Perhaps he would be able to help me stay grounded, in control. He had helped before.

This morning, I was a little heavy in the heart. I was tired from my ordeal at the hospital, to ASSIST, back to the hospital, and back to ASSIST. I just wanted to go back to my life and put all this behind me. I had toast with peanut butter, chewing slowly as I sat at the table. It was dark inside and overcast outside. I swallowed the bread as my mind thought about leaving. Was I ready? Could I control the neighbors' commands? I didn't know for sure. I just wanted home.

Outside, the rain left its stain on the sidewalk that passed by my window. The grass was incredibly green, and the rocks, cool shades of white. I really liked the colors. There hadn't been much in the hospital. I had missed that.

Through the trees, I could see my office window, where I had worked, where I had performed my old routine. Would I be able to return to work, go back to the way things were? I should be over there working right now, not sitting here at ASSIST trying to remain calm. I was trying to be patient as I waited for word that I could leave.

The doctor came in and gave me the news. I could leave, as long as they could contact my husband. They wanted Jim to keep the medicine out of my reach for a while. I agreed. I just wanted home.

I went outside in the rain and walked to the shelter. Rain fell, wiping away the strain of living, cleaning the landscape. I sat on the wooden picnic bench and had a smoke. I was going home soon and I couldn't wait. I was impatient to get back to life.

I thought about the week of turmoil. I had taken an overdose, been hospitalized, been through so many doctors and therapists trying to determine how best to help. In the end, the change in medicine and my desire to fight the neighbors were what helped. I took a drag of my cigarette and blew the smoke out into the rain.

I watched bumblebees on purple flowers. They were still collecting nectar even in the light rain. I smelled the wet scent of milkweeds, the soaking wet grass, and breathed it all in. I was so glad to be outside and not locked up. I didn't want to go back in.

I thought about my family, all my boys. How I loved them and wished I could give them a stable mother. It was so hard to handle the neighbors' rantings, I wanted to end that pain inside somehow. I wanted to be brave and do the right thing, do it the right way.

I didn't want to die. I just wanted to end the tirade in my head. It wasn't really neighbors, if I was honest. It was self-doubt that was ruminating and disturbing me. If I could only find a way to end my despair and anxiety, perhaps it would diminish.

A new client who had just arrived, came out to smoke. He was young, in his twenties. He had curly hair and a red beard. He sat by me and shattered the silence with questions. He had a lot of energy and he wanted to know everything about me. I was short with my answers, trying not to encourage him. He sucked his cigarette down to the filter and then jumped up and walked down the gravel path, back to the house.

I lit another cigarette and looked up at the trees. They reached out of the ravine, their trunks like gray rays shooting from the ground. I watched their leaves turn in the mist, watched them seem to dance in the rain. I wished that I felt like dancing. My husband loved to dance, but we seldom went out because of my anxiety.

I stood, stubbed out my cigarette, and then threw it into the bucket of butts. I walked slowly through the sprinkles. I felt the cold droplets spritzing me, felt them touch my skin and drip off. I was okay with the rain.

I went inside and gathered my few things. I packed them into a red bag and a paper bag. I was ready to go home. I called Jim and told him I was coming home and asked when he could pick me up. He would come at lunch-time. The doctor came in wearing horn-rimmed spectacles, and a tie over a too-tight oxford. He was also young.

"Are you able to keep yourself safe?" he waited for me to answer. He didn't look certain.

I nodded. I was going home even if the neighbors were still telling me to end my life. He didn't need to know that.

"Can your husband take your medications and hand them out to you so you can be safe?" he asked.

I nodded again telling him, "I am feeling much better, more in control of myself."

The doctor nodded. A few more questions and then he agreed I could leave when I was ready. I smiled and walked him to the door of my room. He left and went through the employees-only door. He would sit at his desk and write up a summary report saying that I was better.

Good, I thought. *I am almost home.*

CHAPTER NINETEEN

It was just eight days since I had taken the pills. Over a week since I had given in to the neighbors' demands. It felt longer. Time locked away seemed to expand, grow into long minutes of being stuck. The time seemed so long, too many different beds that hurt my back. Too many people checking up on me, watching me, telling me what to do or what to take. I was ready to go home.

I didn't feel different. I was taking a higher dose of an antipsychotic and was no longer on one of the antidepressants. Maybe I did feel a little better. I wasn't constantly thinking of a way to end my life. The neighbors weren't quite as demanding either. Yes, I had changed a bit.

I waited by the glass door for my husband to arrive. He pulled in at around quarter to twelve and I opened the door for him. He helped me gather my few bags and then came back to get my medications. They wouldn't let me hold onto them. Precautions that went away when I got back home.

It felt weird to be driving down the road, passing cars filled with people living through normal moments, doing normal things. I felt like I had been gone for a month and the world should have stopped. But it never did, for anyone. Look at Robin Williams. He was gone. People posted blurbs about him on the Internet. People shook their heads and looked sad, but the world went on. People kept their usual routines of work, home, and play. The earth still spun, and the days grew shorter.

It was raining when we got home. Jim helped me get my bags and we went inside. He still had to work, so we sat in the living room. I read a book while he worked at his computer. Soon, he took a break and we stood up together. He kissed me hard, and I kissed him back urgently.

We ended up in bed, wrapped around each other, lost in the moment of rediscovering ourselves. It had been a long time since we had been passionate with one another. It was wonderful. I held him close to me and he held me closer. We were back.

I thought of all the times we had waited to be together. When we were just dating, all we wanted was to sleep side-by-side. Because of my illness, we had been away from each other too often. Nights in strange beds, nights without each other to hold had made it difficult.

The day quickly passed, time for us to pick up Michael from school. My little boy burst through the school door, holding onto his dad's hand, and rushing to the car through the rain. He didn't notice me in the car until the door was open. He grinned and piled in with enthusiasm. He clung to my hand and I held his tight.

He had made me a bracelet and he slid it onto my wrist. It was rainbow-colored, with beads brightly adorning a green pipe-cleaner. I loved it, even though one end was sharp and picky. We drove to the store to buy him some school supplies and some food at a grocery store. It was a normal moment that I savored.

Soon enough, we slipped back into the comfortable routine that most households shared. Dinner, cleaning, time spent with the family, bedtime. I tucked my son into bed after his injection and kissed him on both of his cheeks. He padded up the ladder to his loft bed and I covered him with his snowman sheet and blanket.

"Good night," I said to his still body.

"Goodnight Mommy," he whispered, curling into his pillow.

I left the hall light on and went to the familiar bed I shared with my husband. He was reading and I curled up next to him. I had taken an extra antipsychotic pill when we had gotten home and I was starting to feel its effect. Things in my mind seemed slower, I was calmer. I was safe. I pulled the covers up and put an arm around my husband. I loved him. I just wished things in my mind could always be this quiet.

He kissed me good night and rubbed my back. He was gentle and loving. I hugged and kissed him back. I put on my CPAP and fan. Back in my own bed, I stretched and felt luxurious in the cluttered room, my own space. I was back and I wanted to stay here always.

I was going to be alright. My story was of strength. I had battled hard with life but was still standing. And my family was all safe. No one was hurt. I shook my head to dispel the laughter that taunted me. The neighbors could laugh, but I was okay. Their laughter was an echo of insecurity raining down on me. I had a roof over my head. I was safe. And I was going to keep on living. There really was no choice in the matter. I wanted to be here. Wanted to watch my boys grow into men with their own lives. Wanted to hold Jim's hand for another twenty-five years and more. I deserved that. So did he.

Strength through Laughter

The voices pulled at me, laughed
at my desire to be free. Me,
the suburban housewife
raging at the noise in my head,
the loud threats, the angry chatter,
the rattles inside that filled

me with dread, and at times
wishing to be dead. But I also
had strength! A battle burned
inside, lit up my reserves,
depleted my senses at times
but I had ever managed
to turn the tides of the war
and find victory back home.
I leaned into my husband's arm,
breathed in the charm
of his scent, the life we were meant
to share. We had a rare love,
tousled hair, whirlwind kind of way,
and the steady beat that pulsed
through our days apart
until we could find our way
back to the start again of our beautiful marriage,
back to the days united, delighted
when we found ourselves joined
in the satisfaction of normalcy
In the freedom of truly living.

I smiled as I snuggled under the covers. I was alive and doing my best. And that was okay. That was more than okay. I was strong and capable.

Soon, I would taking my youngest son to and from school again. Summer was coming to a close and I had decided. I decided that even though the neighbors were there, I would not listen. I would go on, and remain focused on the moment. I would continue to provide a safe, nurturing environment where my son could live, without my focusing on the noisy neighbors. I delighted in the details of his days, his genuine love for each moment. I would learn from him as well.

The neighbors were just on the other side of the wall, nothing new, just a lot of noise. I chose to ignore them. Sometimes that worked.

"Dear Lord, thank you for my life," I prayed. "Thank you for my life." Life is just a simple thing, a way of living. Just trying to bring a little more light into the world. And I did bring forth more light. There were good moments, ones that overcame the noise of the neighbors. I curled up next to my husband and slept.

CHAPTER TWENTY

Fall came with the arrival of my son's first day of school. I took his picture in front of the house just before we got in the car. He grinned back at me, his knapsack flung over a shoulder. First grade for him now. He was getting so big.

The shots that he took each night were helping him grow and he was catching up to the kids in his class. The nightly routine didn't scare him anymore. He tensed, and then let me give him the shot. If he could get used to this ordeal, then I would be strong with the neighbors.

I still heard them every day. Heard the sneers, the laughter, the cruel words that spun in my head and hurt. And every day I prayed for them to go away, leave me alone. But they never did.

Fall was here in its golden hues, the oranges, reds, and yellows, alive in the neighborhood trees. I drove past a red maple in brilliant crimson delight. I passed houses with planters still holding on, leftover flowers from summer's days, new mums filling other pots, giving color to the yards.

I dropped my son off, watched him wave to me as he headed into the building. Then, I was driving to work and preparing to help others with mental illness find employment. My job was hard. I wasn't sure if I could continue, but the agency still wanted me.

Days went by and I filled them with projects, meetings, introductions to employers, bringing my son to and from school. Each afternoon, he would burst into the red Beetle Bug, the name we gave to my car. He was filled with the chatter of his days at school and I would delight in the news, in his happiness as I drove him home.

Halloween came and my son dressed up as a firefighter to go trick-or-treating. We walked the neighborhood with him knocking on doors for candy. He would hold my hand between houses and I loved it. The neighbors, the voices I heard so many times each day, were getting loud, but I was able to push past them and stay in the moment. I wished I could end their noise, and wished I could simply make them go away.

November came, and I grew depressed with the cold. Stark outside, no more flowers, pumpkins squashed on the road, stalks of gardens' ghosts of summer gone before. I grew sad with the barren landscape, the bleak trees with no leaves, the brown grassy yards.

The neighbors' noise grew daily and I found it hard to escape them. One day in a meeting at work, I couldn't take the loudness. I tried to focus on the conversation. A doctor was talking about forcing his patient to undergo a treatment. I thought back to the times when I had ECT, not in control of my own body. I went rigid. The neighbors grew loud in laughter. I stood up and walked out of the meeting.

Max, my therapist tried to keep me grounded. We worked on my breathing, on focusing on the environment, the colors, the sounds. Nothing seemed to work. I was scared, tired of fighting, scared to be at work now.

Max

He was a gentle man, had a plan to ground me
from the terror inside. He tried singing to me
of the sands of the beaches in Maine to rid
the pain that seared my soul. He sat me
on the dunes, so soon needing to be found

there, aware of the gulls squawking above,
my love beside me, my boys splashing in the waves.
I braved the despair with Max. He brought
his soothing sounds, his soft voice the favored
choice to relieve the blinding panic, the manic
disturbance deluding me to run. I felt the tiny
rocks ground into the soft packed sand
of the beach, reached my hand into the pebbles
and pulled my fingers out with the bits running
through, sticking myself into a memory
that was like aloe on a sunburned pain.
He was gentle, a harbor to set into
when the waters of my life were crashing,
thrashing and sinking my own ship.
I docked at his shore, more days than
I can count. And he dried my hull,
he didn't ask to rebuild my name,
he knew I still had the frame, the husk
of me still good. He brought me
back to seaworthy and then one day
I had to disembark and set sail
on a different journey. He let me loose
as I went to a Jewish woman with tattoos
and EMDR and to witness
the telling of my truth. I miss Max still,
like that brief escape at the beach
his help like the immeasurable sands
there. I left him in the fall of my life,
with the leaves changing, arranging
my world to be a little more vulnerable,
always knowing I could recall
myself leaving the chair in his room
and grounding myself to the sunshine

pouring over my head on a Maine beach at will.

It got worse and I returned to ASSIST for help. I stayed there at the house, talking with workers, sleeping, worrying. I met with my case worker and decided to give up my job. I made the decision to go back to part-time work with preschoolers at a fitness gym. With the decision made, I felt calmer, able to handle the noise in my head. I walked out back for a cigarette and sat on a bench looking about. The trees were crooked stalks that reached up to dim sunshine. A squirrel flitted about the yard and I watched it carry nuts. Things were calmer in my head, if only I could hold on to this peace.

Things weren't so bad now. I was strong, had been strong enough to get through the noise in my mind. It just wore me down to constantly hear the negative chatter. I blew out a last puff of smoke and crushed the cigarette on the ground. I stood up and walked back inside.

I sat at a table and worked on a jigsaw puzzle. Soft music was playing and a worker came by to share the puzzle with me. It was a quiet moment, the two of us searching for pieces that fit. It was nice to share the quiet with someone, but I missed my husband. I thought I could go home now and prepare for a new job. I went to call Jim and arrange to go home. He was excited that I was coming back. I was glad that he was there for me, again. He was amazing.

Two days later, I started the part-time job at a preschool. It was a different pace, filled with diapers, book readings, and snack times. I fell into the pattern and the days seemed to go by fast.

Winter came, and with it I noticed the beauty of the land. Snow covered the ground, covered the brown grass, hid the dead plants with a stark whiteness I found thrilling. I gathered up our holiday decorations and turned the house into a Christmas scene. My son loved the decorations, and was counting the days until Christmas.

The holidays found me home with all three boys and my husband. We celebrated Christmas morning with presents by the tree and then went to my mother-in-law's home for more gift-giving and a brunch.

I loved watching the boys open the gifts, watching the sparkle in their eyes as they opened them and delighted in each discovery. Michael enjoyed opening his gifts with great gusto and laughter.

And the neighbors were quiet. I reveled in their silence, treasured it, held on to it.

CHAPTER TWENTY-ONE

When January came, I found it harder to focus on the positive. I went to my weekly therapy with Max. I worked. I drove Michael to and from school, but still urt with the noise in my mind.

It grew cold, the wind harsh as I stood outside to have a cigarette. I blew out the smoke in a cloud of breath, felt the wind grate against my face, felt sad that things were getting hard again. My job was getting stressful. The noise of the room was triggering the neighbors' noise and it was hard to cope. Things were getting out of hand again and I didn't know what to do.

I thought back to the retreat house, Alyssum, and wished I could visit. I wondered what it would be like now that there was an addition to the building. Would there be more activities since the space was larger? Did they still go visit the river? Would the river still be there, winding along, waiting for me to visit? Would I find help being in the solitude of the Green Mountains? I went to Max and wept for the lack of control I felt.

With Max, I called my boss and told her that the job was too stressful and I had to end it. My boss was understanding. Now I had to find another job. I had applied to the airport for a customer service position and was waiting to find out if I had gotten it.

Days later, I found out that I had gotten the job and I went for training at the airport. It was a busy place, and I quickly learned the routine. The hours were not great, some early mornings, but I thought I could manage it.

Months later, found me struggling again. Winter was over and spring was here. I found moments to watch leaves come out, flowers open, grass turn green. And I worked.

Spring found me more hopeful that the neighbors would be quieter, a hope I needed to believe in.

The job was getting stressful with customers upset over missing flights, not enough workers scheduled, and chaotic schedules. I decided to leave that job and go back to work at Homegoods.

I called the manager and went to fill out an application.

Soon, I was back at Homegoods working part-time as a cashier. It was good not to be held responsible for others, to do my job, and then leave. I greeted customers, smiled, worked hard when I was there, and then went home to enjoy time with my family.

I recalled one day during the holiday season as a cashier when a woman came to my line.

"Jodi!" The woman smiled and I smiled back, not recognizing her. "Do you remember me?"

"I'm sorry, no." I smiled again.

The woman dug in her purse and pulled out a creased and wrinkled white sheet of paper.

She handed it to me. I looked down at the poem, my name at the bottom.

"We were in the hospital together and one day when I was really sad, you wrote that for me. I have carried it with me these last few years."

I smiled at the woman and scanned her items for sale. It was strange to share a memory with someone I didn't know. I had written so many poems, given so many out. I had created poems for funerals for others, for weddings to celebrate life, reading them aloud as a gift.

Perhaps my life still meant something.

I had decided that I would continue to give, continue

to write poetry, continue living despite the madness in my mind.

The Cashier

Not everyday does a customer surprise me.
I mean, I ring the orders, it borders on dullness
to social gossip with the ladies. Oh there
is fun with my cohorts, the ones that have sparks
in their eyes as we make the registers sing.
One day a small lady came to me. She grinned
and threw up her arms, exclaimed how she missed
me and I didn't know if I knew her.
As I entered her purchases
she pulled a paper out of her purse.
My scratched up handwriting in ink on the page,
a poem I had written about her hope. She kept
it for years in a pocket of her purse. She carried
hope from me I had forgotten. It filled me
with my own purpose, my own love,
my own worthiness to be. I wanted to hold
on to that feeling, the healing that I helped
and savored from our meeting, this wondrous
greeting here in the retail store. I played
the rest of my shift with the three sisters,
Deb, Faye, and Cindy. We laughed
in the aisles as I put back returns
With a feverish delight to be living still.

Michael had his eighth birthday party, a Star Wars Lego theme. I organized for weeks, bought decorations, party favors, and games for the kids to play. I made a Death Star pinata for the kids to whack at. The party went smoothly, kids running about with light sabers made out of noodles, and bubbles blowing about the room. The Star Wars theme played in the background while the kids played games. We brought out colored balloons and let them try to whack them from one side of the rented gym to the other. It was a festive occasion and I enjoyed the smiles on my son's face.

The next day we piled into the Beetle Bug and drove to Hampton Beach for two nights away. My husband's sister, Beth came along and it was fun riding in the car in anticipation of getting to the beach.

We arrived early and walked along the sandy shore. I took off my shoes and walked in the water, slipping past rocks, looking for shells, exploring the waves. The sun shone down and I lifted my arms to capture the warmth inside. The neighbors were not loud and I was happy to be in the moment.

Later, we checked into a motel and walked the strip, grabbing a quick lunch, and letting Michael play in the arcade. I played Skee-Ball with my family, tossed the balls down the lane, laughed as one tucked into a fifty-point spot. It reminded me of past family vacations with my older boys, and even farther back when I was with my own parents and siblings. How we all spent time rolling the balls down the lanes, laughing at the joy of the moment. Peace was here and I savored it.

That night we drove to Kittery in Maine and went to a Trading Post filled with stuffed animals, moose, beaver, deer, elk, fox, and coyotes. We bought Michael a sweatshirt for the Whale Watch we planned the next day.

Dinner found us at the Weathervane. I had a plate of piled-up clam bellies. Beth put on a bib and ate lobster. Michael tried Calamari, fried squid, and he loved it. Jim had scallops and clams. We enjoyed the meal and I was thankful that the noise in my head was just a buzzing, no voices piercing reality.

The next day, we began the morning by walking along the beach. Michael played in the waves and I found it calming to sit on the sand watching his happiness. He jumped the small waves on the shore and raced back out with the receding water. I pressed my hands into the sand, squeezing the wetness into fists, imprinting myself on the beach, on the moment.

Jim and Beth walked by the rocks and took pictures. I went out in the water with Michael and we jumped the waves. I was relaxed, happy, and didn't want it to end. After a couple hours, we went back to the room and changed.

Jim, Beth, and Michael went off on a whale watch while I walked the strip. I was too seasick to go, so I went into stores and looked at the souvenirs, the shirts, the shells, the flip-flops. I made my way down the strip to the casino and went in to play bingo. Two hours later, I came out with thirty dollars more than I started with.

I walked in the sun back to the room, enjoying the strangers about me, noticing their outfits and lack of outfits. I closed my eyes and raised my face to the sun to capture more of its warmth. I was happy.

Later, the crew came back from the whale watch, tired and soaked. The water had been choppy and Michael had gotten sick three times on the boat. They had seen whales but were just glad to be back.

Beth and I walked down to the strip and brought back supper. I had a lobster roll and it was really good. Michael had a peanut butter and jelly sandwich which he loved. We ate and then walked the strip again.

The lights of the strip were on and the neon glowed all

around us. It was fun to be in the crowd, stopping to look in stores, to play games in the arcade, to observe the people doing the same thing. I felt glad to be alive. I was excited to be in the moment. And the neighbors' noise was low. It was starting to grow but I pushed past them, concentrating on the sights and the sounds by the shore. I knew that I would always hear them, they were all of my self-doubt, fear turned into a symptom that I couldn't control. But I was taking steps to keep going beyond their noise, beyond the fear. If only I could keep fighting, life would be better. I was going to keep trying.

The next day, the rain came down hard. We drove to the USS Albacore, a submarine now a museum, and wandered through it. Michael stood by the periscope and looked outside. We took pictures and commented about how small and enclosed the space was that housed so many men.

After the submarine we made our way to York Beach, Maine. We stopped by the water's edge and parked, watching the rough sea as it stormed the shore. Jim got out and took pictures of the big waves. Then we drove to the Short Sands and parked.

The rain continued to pour down and we ran to the arcade and let Michael play some games, hoping the rain would subside. We all played Skee-Ball again and laughed as we rolled balls down the lanes.

The rain did not let up as we left the arcade and raced across the street to the taffy store. Out front, we stood in the crowd watching workers make the taffy, stretching it out on the machine, pouring some into pans. It was wet all about us and not very comfortable.

Soon, we piled back in the Bug and began our journey home. The rain came down in sheets and when we got on the interstate, big trucks made it impossible to see through the spray from their wheels. My anxiety crept up as Jim passed the trucks, but I continued to apply calming breaths.

We stopped in West Lebanon, New Hampshire for lunch. The rain stopped and the sun came out. I crawled into the small backseat with Michael for the last leg of the trip. We dropped Beth off and made it home, vacation over, normalcy back.

I remembered the beach, watching the waves, sitting in the sand. It was a good memory. I thought things were going much better. I was still working through the noise in my mind. People at work were kind, and I was capable of doing my job.

Goldenrod

I want to reach out to touch
the Goldenrod where the taffy circles
On the metal pulling it apart and crowds watch
As the baker pries new batches out of the pans,
To pack it on the machine that wraps it in paper.
The sweet sugar smell brings also the salt, the sand,
And the memories drifting back
of a young family playing by the ocean
With my dad still here.
I want to see the white clapboards again,
And the yellow sign,
And inhale the diner food of gravy and fries,
And walk down the sidewalk
With the gulls and the tourists
And the windows with the cheap glitzy
Covered souvenirs I cried for.

I long to drape an arm between my mom's,
Both of us in half shirts with "York" in pink written across,
walking down walks with sunburns and freckles.
I want to bring Jim again for the first time
With my family, have them meet him, the young teen
I fell for, me chasing him in the surf,
The white foam coating us with the season.
I want my children to walk into the Fun-O-Rama
And stand beside their Papa once more
inserting quarters into the Skee-Ball games
To pitch the hard balls into the holes
For a chance to savor victory as champion roller.
I want to roll onto a beach towel, dig toes
Into the cool particles of the beach
And remind myself that seasons still change
And it is now summer again
only my dad isn't here,
won't be there when we go soon... but...
Perhaps I can breathe in his life lived so well.
Savor his passions and the things that brought him smiles,
Like the goldenrod.
All of us scattered before the window
Watching the taffy turn, the changing colors,
The stretching out of a summer week that we'll re-member,
hold onto, a week that changes the way we live.

Michael would be starting second grade soon. I had ordered his uniform shirts and they had come in. He was almost ready after a week of camp at Red Rock Park. He swam, hiked, kayaked, and played in the woods with the other campers.

There was a lot to be thankful for, a lot to look forward to. Hope was all around us and I wrapped myself in it like a blanket, willing myself to be positive about life. In times like these, I looked back thankfully at the many hardships I had overcome. Good and bad things had happened but I was still fighting. It wasn't over yet.

CHAPTER TWENTY-TWO

September came with the slow change of color in the environment. Trees once pure green were now scattered with yellows and oranges. Some of the leaves were on the ground and the squirrels made tracks through the leaves as they gathered up their winter's stores to bury.

I continued to work and I helped Michael with his homework. I spent nights cooking dinners for my family and watching TV shows in the evening. The neighbors were loud and I would shake my head to dispel their noise. It didn't always work.

My husband would hold me and whisper lovingly into my ear.

"Listen to my words not the hurt you hear," he would say brushing back my hair behind an ear. "I love you."

So I would hold on to that hope that things would improve. I went to work and I helped my family. I was thinking about becoming a substitute teacher to make more money and I felt good about that.

But, the neighbors were getting louder. Hateful words were pounded into my ears so many times a day. I couldn't escape them.

"You're no good. We hate you. You should kill yourself." Again and again the taunting and trappings that hurt, lowered my moods, made me want to hide.

One day at work, I had to leave early because it was so loud I couldn't concentrate. I left and made it home to Jim who held me and kissed me and told me how special I was to him. I clung to him and sobbed, while the noise circled around me and made me despair.

Then two days later, I called into work, said I wasn't

feeling well. They told me to get better. Jim didn't want me to stay home alone while he was at work, so I went to my mother's in Williston.

I stopped at the CVS pharmacy and picked up some medicine. The neighbors were hurtful, loud, angry. I shook my head, tried to deny their existence, just another noise that didn't affect me. But it did and I couldn't seem to focus on anything else.

At my mother's house I sat with her while we watched the Pope on television. He was speaking to the United Nations. He was here in the United States and so many people had come out to see him. He was loved by so many.

The voices were so loud that it was hard for me to hear what the Pope was saying. Tears fell from my eyes and my mother told me to call my doctor. I couldn't get a hold of him so I called Crisis. I reached out for help with my mother's support.

A meeting was set for noon and I drove back to my house to pack some things in case they wanted me to stay at ASSIST again. My mother drove me to the meeting. In the car we passed the trees, greens, and yellows, and oranges--a sun out to brighten up the fall's display. College kids crossed the street in packs, bikers rode alongside the cars up the hill, and I stared out at all the living going on.

We turned down Pine Street and made our way to Crisis. Patti, my case manager, met us at the door and we all walked into a small room with many chairs in a circle. There was little talk. They asked if I thought ASSIST would be a good place for a little while. I didn't know, I just wanted to decrease the noise in my head, stop the death thoughts.

They showed me to a room. A twin bed with a yellow, flowered bedspread was in one corner, a white, wicker seat across from it. I pulled down the blinds that faced a parking lot where people were gathered talking and realized, I am here now.

My mother left and I set about getting distracted. I spoke with the nurse, the workers. I did a jigsaw puzzle. I wanted to scream, wanted to run down the street with my hands in the air proclaiming my helplessness. But I picked up a newspaper and read. I went out to the backyard and had a smoke.

Tall yellow flowers filled the ditch beside a picnic table. Bees flew between the petals. I watched them land on the flowers and make their way from one to another. The grass was still green and the sun was out. I breathed in and out with the cigarette, calming myself as I watched and listened to the bees.

Over the weekend, we went apple picking and I saw a bees' nest in the barn. Bees flew in between the plastic compartments and fed the young. They were busy with their way of life. A small tube opened to the outside and they came and went throughout the day.

We had taken a tractor ride to the orchard and picked Macs. Great big ones covered the trees and the apples were just the right height for Michael to reach. We bit into crisp apples and sucked the juice as we picked.

Now, I was here at ASSIST and it was quiet.

Quietness

Back in the dilemma of my delusions,
the simple conclusion that I am better
off away sometimes. I find panic
in my heart, a start that fuels fears
and I escape into the outside

with smoke on my breath
and the voices only whispered
thoughts in my ears of death.
It is still quietness with the fume of white
surrounding my body, my soul
wrapped in the Band-Aids
of a system that doesn't always heal.
I feel like I am being ripped open,
a token toy pulled out of the game,
the claw of life. Am I to be
discarded and hidden away when the despair
tears at my weakness?
I am a mess and I stand with the ravine before me,
The den again with foxes, the slyness of my disease
That makes me believe I am really no one.

At least the house was quiet. Voices slammed within my head and hurt. I tried to ignore them, distract with some writing. Anything to help. I was getting weaker and beginning to listen to their demands. Were they my demands? Did a part of me really want to die? I wanted the noise to stop but I wanted to keep on and live.

My husband and Michael came to visit. They brought my medicine and some Diet Coke.

We sat in my room and talked. Michael told me about his day at the apple orchard on a field trip. He wrote me a note, "I love you sooooooooooooooooooooooooooooo much!" with lots of o's and commas in between each of the o's. It was really sweet.

Soon they were leaving and I was left alone again. I wondered how I'd get through the night without my husband's arms around me. I thought that maybe I would call him and talk to him.

Dinner came and I had pizza with a group of strangers. Silence greeted me at the table. No one had anything to say. People chewed their pizza, drank their drinks, and then shuffled off to their rooms. Was I going to make it here?

I walked outside and sat at the picnic table. A breeze lifted my hair, and I raised my head to catch its movement. Outside, the flowers swayed, the squirrels clamored about, and I watched the sky as it darkened. I was at least glad to be somewhere with a view, not the sterile environment of a hospital floor. I watched as the clouds covered the last bit of sun. It was heading toward darkness and I really felt alone.

My husband sent me a note that made me smile. He was always thinking of me. That was important. The noise in my head was just that. Noise to escape from. Small moments of breathing, talking with Jim, writing.

I just had to ignore the rest.

I had taken a Lorazepam and things were a bit calmer inside. My thoughts were muddled but that was okay for right now. The new increased dosage of medicine would make me more tired, but I could get through it if only things would become quieter in my head. I needed quiet. I would hold on to that, and for now, seek to distract.

Night came and I put on my CPAP. I drifted off in a fog of Loxapine-induced sleep. It came with respite from the voices but brought on nightmares that were hard to shake. I would wake up, turn, toss, roll again, and then fall back to sleep.

In the morning the sun was out. It was Saturday. My husband called and asked me to come home. I told him I wanted that more than anything. I spoke with the workers in the office, told them I was feeling better and felt able to go home. They agreed and Jim came to pick me up before it could be revised.

I pressed my face to the passenger window to feel the sun as we drove home. It was nice and quiet in my head. I squeezed Jim's hand. He smiled at me to show he loved me. I thought maybe I was going to make it.

CHAPTER TWENTY-THREE

I walked about my home looking at it as if I'd been away for a long time, not just twenty-four hours. I looked at the photos on the wall, the portrait of a girl leaning on a pillar. Was she dreaming? I looked at the painting of another girl with her hair blowing back, was she on a bike? It was a head and chest shot so it was hard to know.

She looked as if she was pedaling with her hands out before her holding on to something. I walked down the hall and stared at Sappho, the first woman poet in a frieze we had hanging there. It was a side view. She had strong sharp features, a sharp nose, long hair frizzed out behind her. Strong women on my walls, each dreaming, each holding a part of what I wanted. To live freely.

I wanted to be bold and keep my head up. I wanted to dream longer. I wanted to be careless and free outside, in nature. I wanted to be rid of the voices that haunted me. I wasn't sure just how to do that though.

Later, Michael came bursting into the room, his happiness spilling out in a rush of words that greeted me from the door. We talked about his time with his aunt and how we were getting ready to go on a hike in Stowe. We climbed into the red bug and drove to meet up with the other Cub Scouts and parents. On the way, we stopped and bought drinks and popcorn for the road trip.

It was pleasant with the sun shining, the radio playing, and the voices in my head just a murmur. I distracted them with talk to my husband and son. I listened to the radio. I watched the changing colors of the trees sliding by.

At Stowe, we parked and all got out to meet up with others gathered for the hike. Michael was excited to see his friends. The scout leader gave a speech and then we headed down the trail to Bingham Falls. Packed dirt, fallen leaves, and twigs were everywhere. The sun came through in slants. I tired easily but kept up. We came to a steep descent with rock stairs and proceeded to climb down slowly. There were nineteen kids and a handful of adults to manage them but we all made it.

Down by the river, some of the kids jumped into a small waterhole and kicked and laughed. I sat on a large boulder and watched them. Michael clamored up and down the boulders with Jim's help. I watched as the pack moved down the slide of water over rocks.

I had decided to stay where I was and wait. I noted the water, knew it was cold, and watched it lap against the rocks. I listened to the falls tumbling from my left up river. Some older kids were flying a drone and videoing their friends jumping off big rocks into the water.

It reminded me of being by the river at Alyssum. How I missed the farmhouse and the peer support workers who had helped me through some of my symptoms. The comradeship, the encouragement, no stigma. I looked at the river, the pools so deep with boulders beneath the water. Someone else's baggage dropped? I wished I knew how to go back in my mind and be there.

I sat on a large flat rock and watched as the pack turned around a bend and were out of sight. I sat back against another rock and breathed in and out. The neighbors were bothering me but I just noticed them and didn't judge. I could handle this. I could handle this.

By the River

I watched my boy seek out the adventure
of the day with his troop as I sat behind
on a flat boulder, the sun hitting me
with splendid light. I lazed by the river,
reminded of the hurt I had thrown,
alone by the retreat house, into
the running water. I watched
the movement now, swirling
about the rock island I sat upon.
Older boys were flying a drone,
shaping memories to take back
to their other life. I looked
at the trees guarding the edge
of the current, tall pines standing by
the rocky shore. I wanted more
of this life. This right here!
Near to the essence of what
life should be, the sun
in my eyes, and the surprise
of the day the sweet-scented
purpose of nature-filled moments.

Minutes passed. I heard them before I saw them. Kids were splashing in the water. Some of the boys were climbing over the rocks as they made their way back to where I sat. Most of the kids were smiling. I liked that. I smiled too. Life could be good. It could be as simple as a hike in the woods by a beautiful falls. It could be good. I just had to reach out and grab hold of the beauty that I found here and turn it inward.

The neighbors laughed, called me stupid, said they were going to kill me. I pushed them away as I saw my man climbing back over rocks to me. I grinned at him and he grinned back, silently mouthing the words, "I love you." I would hold onto those words.

The way back was tough. I wasn't ready for the uphill hike back. It was slow going. I was the last one to make it out of the woods and back to the side of the road. A man had passed me and returned with a solid branch for me to use as a walking stick. I thought that was nice.

We drove home over the Notch, coming down by way of Smugg's on the other side of the mountain. There were many cars and people up there, all enjoying the outdoors. The leaves were changing slowly. In a few weeks it would be lit up like a toddler's crayon drawing, all colors scribbled out on branches, wild and crazy. I hoped that maybe we would come back.

We drove home in the comfort of each other, listening to our Michael chatter, singing to the radio, living in a simple way that brought such joy.

Sunday came and I had to lector at church. I was hearing voices and fought to stay focused when I was up in front of the congregation. I managed to get through it and sit in the pew with my family. After Mass, we taught catechism and then went home to a day of comfort. We ate together, watched football, and played a game of Parcheesi.

That night was a lunar eclipse. We drove out of the city and observed the moon in all its fullness out where the city lights weren't interfering. The moon looked huge and it shone bright. It lit up a pond below, and sparkles rippled on the water. A couple passed our car carrying a blanket and plunged into the dark field. Romance was in the air.

Jim drove me back home so I could watch *Zombie*

Monsters with my sister. Michael and Jim went back out to see if they could see the moon become eclipsed. Every few minutes I would poke my head outside and look up at the moon. Soon I could see it begin to go dark and reddish and called Tammy to come outside. Jim came back with Michael and we all looked up at the moon. Only a crescent was left visible while the rest was all a reddish gray color. Everyone in the neighborhood gathered in the street outside their homes, staring up at something bigger than their lives. The greatness of the moon spilled over us.

It reminded me of the time I had escaped the psychiatric floor as a girl only to play in the snow, enjoying the nature of life with others. Now, as a middle-aged woman, I watched as we all stood on the pavement reaching out towards something beyond each of us. I watched Michael smile up to the light, staring intently. I tried to do the same.

Soon, we went in and to bed. Another day completed with the voices. I snuggled up close to my husband. He held me in his arms, we kissed, we loved, we slept.

Monday came and I went to see Max, my therapist. I stayed for half an hour and we talked about my struggle. I didn't know what would help. We decided to make another appointment on Wednesday. I left feeling a bit disheartened that there wasn't a magic cure for the voices and then I went to volunteer at Michael's school library.

Later that day, Michael said, "Andy, can you believe it that your mother was the librarian who checked out our books? That was cool."

It made me smile at his happiness, his love.

Tuesday, I worked. The neighbors were loud and I stood my ground. I wanted to run, wanted to scream, and I planted my feet on the floor. I checked out customers. I smiled. I rang the register. Later, I patted myself on the back for getting through it. That was something. Wednesday, I couldn't get it together. I cried. I slept. I tossed my head to dispel the voices that drove me crazy. I drove to see Max and cried in his office. I wept for my inability to keep myself safe. I wanted to kill myself. I wanted the voices to go away. I wanted the madness to end. We called Crisis together and made an appointment to go back and talk with them. They said there weren't any beds available at ASSIST, so I went home with my mother. Michael was crying when I left and I didn't want to go back home and confuse him. Mom and I ate, watched a movie, and cried together.

Thursday, I waited for ASSIST to call and tell me a room was available. I called in at work and told them I wouldn't be in until next week. They seemed okay but I wasn't sure. It was what it was. I went shopping with my mom and then she took me out to lunch. We had chicken and avocado sandwiches. Then she drove me home to Jim.

I was so glad to see him. I had missed him more than I could say. I kissed him and sat with him and wished I could be different. But I was who I was. Together we went and picked up Michael. He was surprised to see me but smiled so brightly at me. I wished I could be normal for him.

"Mommy, today at school we prayed for you. We prayed for Michael's mother."

How sweet that he was thinking of me while he was at school. Back at home, ASSIST called. It was time for them to take me back. I would have to stay longer this time and actually come up with some better strategies to help with the voices. I had to try. I had to fight. I had to.

I hugged my husband. I kissed my son. I cried when they left. I told myself that I was doing this to be a better person, to get some relief from the noise. To let others be in charge for a little while so I could heal. I was going to heal. The world was still a joyful place, I just had to find something to cover the darkness that shadowed me. I still had some fight left in me.

Another Twin

The single bed again
carrying my weight
as I danced with fate
in another room without my husband.
Would I wait for help to come?
Peel away from the pain
and numbness that surround?
Could I ground myself
into stability? Flee the feelings
of dying? Trying instead
to find courage through
the loud, dark burden
in my ears. I fear the day
my own strength bleeds out
and I am left to wither
into the emptiness
no longer to live.
I give my all to remain here,
so near to help but
not my family. I will
not run, I will not give in
to the noise, my boys
the answer to why I keep on,
why I need to shake my head
and slap back at the voices

that seem to want me dead.

The night was hard as I struggled to settle in. I paced the floor. I wrote. I typed to Jim. I talked with staff. I took a Lorazepam to calm my thoughts. I ate pasta and drank a Diet Coke. I got through the moments, the minutes, the hours of noise in my head with distractions.

I could hear the other patients watching an action movie in the living room. Some shoot 'em up movie. I wondered if I should go sit and watch it to pass the time. My thoughts were slowing now. I was able to breathe in and out. A calmness was coming over me. Soon, I would try to sleep and things would be better in the morning. I prayed they would.

CHAPTER TWENTY-FOUR

Morning came with the sun shining through the blinds. I lifted them and looked outside at all the color. Shades of green were turning yellow and orange now. Fall was here. A wind blew the trees and I watched them shift their positions, rocking back and forth. I rocked back and forth on the twin bed.

I called my husband and talked with him. He was going to come over with my son and a pizza tonight. I hoped the voices were less then, so I could enjoy their company. Things were loud in my head right now. Just the neighbors again, I thought to myself. Nothing new. They want to have me dead. But why? Why do they want to scare me? What is it that I hate about myself right now? If I could answer that question maybe they wouldn't be so loud in my head.

I went outside and sat on a bench. I lit a cigarette and inhaled the smoke, blowing it out in a deep breath. Again and again. I sat and inhaled, blowing out pain and frustration with the smoke. It was a cool morning, windy. I looked across the parking lot to ASSIST. Staff workers were in the windowed office talking. Patients were still asleep or in their room. It was quiet and I liked the silence. I shook my head to void the negative talk coming from my mind. The outside was clear, my insides were confused. I shook my head again and went inside.

I sat down on the twin bed and wrote. I looked at the room with no pictures, the room I was staying in. The walls were a muted yellow. A wicker chair with a green cushion was pushed in a corner by a desk. The twin bed that I sat down on was covered in a blue comforter. Metal shelves were against one wall. And the windows let in the sun. The sunlight was good.

I looked outside and watched the leaves moving. They swelled up and down on their branches. White rocks lined the ground. I thought back to the big boulders I had climbed on at Bingham Falls. These were small replicas of those, but I really could remember being in nature, remember the feel of the hard rock I sat against with the sun on my face.

I looked at the grass turning brown, the leaves changing to colors of yellow and orange but still so much green left. It was the beginning of Autumn, yet warm enough to go sit outside and feel the sun on my face. Still time to explore.

I wished to be back at Alyssum, now. To be at the retreat house with the leaves colored, scattered beside the banks of the river that willingly took my pain with the rocks I threw into its waters. An endless churning from the top of the mountains to that narrow valley in Rochester. Was Ladybug still accompanying a lonely client outside? Was the dog siding up to relieve the ache inside another lost soul? Were the peer support workers still encouraging, sharing in compassionate conversations?

The neighbors laughed at me, caused me pain. I shook my head to scatter their thoughts. I was in control, I was here breathing in the day and looking to find some coping skills. I would go sit with a staff member, talk, try to find comfort in the normalcy of a sunny day. Nothing bad was going to happen today. I was safe from harm. If only I could remember that. If only.

I recalled when I first began hearing them as a teenager up in the islands on Lake Champlain. I didn't tell anyone for fear that I would be locked up. I went months without speaking of the scariness that permeated every part of my day. I held on to Jim but wouldn't tell him what was going on. Now, many people knew about the neighbors that invaded my mind. And they still loved me, still fought for me. Helped me fight the battle.

I was tired of fighting but what else was there to do? I didn't want to curl up in a ball and die. I just wanted some quiet time in my head. Was that so wrong? I prayed to God for healing, I yelled at God for my pain. I thought I would call the priest and see if he could come and visit. Maybe that would help.

Thinking of my priest, I remembered Michael. He was going to make his First Communion this year. This weekend was his Rite of Acceptance where he would stand in front of the church congregation and be blessed and prayed over. He was excited to be taking this next step in his faith and I was proud of the wonderful, sweet, holy boy that he had become.

I wanted to be there in May when he walked down the aisle to receive Jesus into his body and soul. I wished the neighbors would be gone by then. They brought everything down, made me want to destroy myself just to end the tirade that played out in my head. Just thinking of them as the neighbors used to help, I wasn't sure if it was still helping or not.

I thought back to my time at the retreat house. Back again to Alyssum where I really began to share my grief, my pain, my anger. I had strength to open up and let all the pain out. I had dealt with the raw pain of emotion that consumed me and found me wanting to fight for life. A real life with Jim and my boys. Now I was here, still fighting over the leftover traumas that sucked me in with command hallucinations. They ordered me to kill myself. They told me I was worthless. They said they were coming to get me. Things they had been saying for over twenty years. It was still difficult to hear it as if someone else was in the room. I would look about the room and realize I was alone, there was no one there talking, only the voices magnified in my ears.

The retreat house had brought me the will to fight, to keep on. And it had been in such a beautiful environment. The river that flowed seemed to call to me to visit, beckon me to sit by its side and watch it go. I could take things out and throw them like the rocks I dropped into the water and let them flow away beneath the current.

I imagined sitting by the side of the river now. Sitting on the pebbled side, my feet forming over the rocks, my back against a large boulder, my bottom on the smooth stones that littered the banks. I could feel the sun on my face, hear the birds as they sang to each other, feel the wind pressing itself against me, holding me up, giving me the courage to sit still and face the demons that attacked.

Now, I was here at ASSIST, away from the river, but I could still conjure it up. I could still sit by its side and visit in my mind. I saw the farmer's field littered with clay shells from his son's practice. I saw myself side-stepping mounds of manure, and stepping into the fresh tilled soil heading to the river. I passed the cows in the barn, their mooing a greeting. And the sun pressed down, warmed me up, kept me company in my isolation. To the river where I could let go of hurts and scream if I chose.

So I sat, in my mind, by the river and watched the current moving. Rocks stood out and the water just coursed around them, ever flowing. I imagined the geese that would come and land on the water, squawk at me for being there, then preen themselves. I thought of the sun above warming, a light in a darkened mind. I lifted my face and pretended to feel the warmth from the sun. I was calming down, the neighbors weren't so loud.

I couldn't scream now but I could pretend. I could close my eyes and be reminded of being by the river and throwing those rocks into the waves, dropping the heaviness like the weight that pressed down from the guilt and pain of living this life. I could practice being in the moment and breathing. I could try to be still and surround myself with nature's remedies that seemed to help so much.

In the afternoon, I met with staff and worked on coping skills. We made a list of all the things I could do to distract from the noise in my head. No easy fix, just get preoccupied with something else. So I wrote out a list, tried my hand at a puzzle, wrote, napped, talked with staff, kept up my head while inside it, I screamed back at the noise and confusion that muddied my thoughts.

People on Facebook had said kind words and prayers for me. I needed to read that, know that I made a difference in others lives and that they were thinking of me in my difficult time.

People cared. I would too.

Outside, it was getting cool. The wind was sharp. I sat outside and smoked. Beside me, I noticed bright red dots on a tree that were moving. As I got closer I noticed the dots were hundreds of red bugs, all clinging together at the bottom of a dead tree. They moved about on top of each other, all around the tree. They were pretty, a nice color to add to the day. I stayed back from them in case they swarmed, curious at the brightness. A bumblebee stopped in front of me. Did it think I was a flower in my burgundy sweater? It buzzed off and I breathed in and out again and again.

Jim would be coming to see me soon. He would bring something to eat and a visit with my son. We would sit and talk and he would hold me. That was something to look forward to.

A respite from the noise in my head, time spent with an ally. My therapist had said he was an ally as well. Said I had many of them all wanting to make things better. If only someone knew how to void the voices from my mind, make it quiet, make it joyful. Perhaps my priest would have a better idea.

I thought about being anointed again. I had been anointed many times, and it always seemed to help. A confession and then absolution and then an anointing of the sick to heal. Yesterday I said a rosary with my grandmother's beads. My mother had given them to me and I had clung to them in the spare room, meditating on the prayers as my hands clasped each bead.

I thought I was in love with Jesus. Thought that He could help. Thought that there was a time when I would have truly believed that He wanted to help. Did He now? How could I feel at peace when I was so hurting? Prayers were meditative and helped distract. I would ask Jim for a bible.

Tonight, I would see Jim and it would be wonderful. He would hold my hand and look at me as if I was special, like I mattered. And I would hold him back and look at him with all the love that I felt for this dear sweet man.

In February, we would celebrate twenty-seven years of marriage. Twenty-seven years of living together. He had helped even before we were married. He would hold me when we were dating and I would cry and cry. Most nights ended our dates with my weeping, tired, not wanting to go on. He would hold me, brush my hair, hold my hand, whisper love to me. And he still was doing that. He was an amazing man with so much love to share. I wanted to share more of life with him, and wanted the amazing times to be closer together. I was in love. If only I could get beyond the voices and the crazy self-talk that defeated me.

I knew that the talking that I did to myself was negative and not good. I would put a stop to it. I would say, no more! I would give love to me like I showered on others. I gave my heart freely to so many people but not to me. Treated myself like dirt, like nothing, like unworthy to be with. I would begin with a new mantra.

"I am good enough. I am special. I am worth living." I would repeat this everyday until it became a part of me that I could believe. I needed to say it enough times so that I could begin to believe it. I would start now.

CHAPTER TWENTY-FIVE

My mother said that when I was a child I used to sit on a stool and sing. My father would laugh and smile and I would clap my hands and sing to my family. That was a joyful memory. I imagined what that must have been like for the family. Such a young innocent child reaching out in song to give such a gift to them. If only I could think of myself as that innocent child, one that Jesus loved, one that needed only to find some kind of peace and acceptance to get better.

For if I could only accept that I was hearing the neighbors, maybe they wouldn't be so powerful. They weren't a real threat, only my actions could make my life worse. I need only to stop listening to their demanding, negative talk. Could I do that? Could I stand my ground and face the day with the screams and nonsense as background noise? Was I still as brave as my husband said I was?

At 4:30 p.m. my husband brought our son with him to visit. We went into my room and had fish sandwiches and sodas. Michael talked about his day. He said that he told his teacher that his mom was away.

"I asked her, 'Do you know why my eyes are watering?'" And he told her that his mother was away. Tonight he was going to spend the night with aunt Tammy. That would cheer him up.

We visited for an hour, talking, holding hands. Michael played on my computer while I talked with Jim. The voices were loud but I shook them off, concentrating on the family of love in front of me. I hugged tight to Michael, told him I loved him, held him while he squeezed me back.

Soon, they were leaving and I was alone. I tried to do

a puzzle. I wrote. I talked with staff. I took my medicine
and talked on the computer to Jim. The noise in my head
was pressing in, making me want to act on their demands
to kill myself. If I died would the voices be gone for good?
At a cost to my family though. I loved my family and didn't
want to be away from them.

I wrote some more and then curled into bed after taking the medicine. The medicine knocked me out, made me
fall into a dream-filled state. Such vivid dreams. I awoke in
the morning, shaking.

I showered and had breakfast and waited for Jim to
pick me up. He came and took me to the doctor's office.
My blood pressure was high and they wanted to see me. At
the doctor's, my pressure was normal. They looked up the
increase in my medication that helped with the voices and
high blood pressure was a side effect.

I was told to check my pressure every day for a month
and then come back to see him.

Jim and I drove to our house. We were alone. Michael
was having breakfast with aunt Tammy and cousin Lynd-
sie. We went into the bedroom and kissed. Jim pulled off
my shirt, undid my bra and pressed my skin against his.
We held on to each other skin-to-skin for a long time. We
kissed some more and then made slow gentle love.

Untitled

For too long the voices' choice
to end my life was the noise
that divided me from my boys
I hold dear
but I am worth more than
the chore of listening

to their demands, I understand
I have a disease, life is not easy
but I still want to live
for I am worth more
than the loud
tragic assault in my head.
I deserve
to be more instead
of the less messiness
that sometimes consumes
my all.

After, he held me again in his arms, brushed my hair out of my face and whispered, "I love you." I squeezed tight to him and stayed there safe in his arms. The voices hurled threats at me, I shook my head and held on tight to Jim. I was safe. Only I could act on the voices' demands. And I didn't want to die.

Later, we dressed and went to Costco to get sandwiches for the potluck tomorrow at church. We walked slowly about the store holding hands, looking at things, talking. I didn't want it to end.

Soon, we were back in the car and driving back to ASSIST. I was there now, writing. It was a cool day, with a bright sun. A day good for fleece. I was wrapped in a fleece jacket as I sat typing. An art group was coming up and I wanted to join in. Wanted to distract from the noise in my head in any way that helped. I was strong. I was a fighter.

"I am worth living. I am worth living. I am worth living." I said aloud to the room.

I would say it again and again until I believed it. I looked out the window, watched the trees dance in the wind, watched the greens, and yellows, and oranges spin on the branches, watched the faded grass bend with the wind. I was in the moment and it was okay. I was okay. I stood to go make some lunch.

CHAPTER TWENTY-SIX

I walked to the store with a staff member, they didn't want me to be alone yet. As I walked, I listened to him tell of his time on Shepherdson Six when he was ill. He had heard voices and was prescribed Risperdal for it. Over time he was able to come off it and not hear them anymore. I had had times when I didn't hear things, but lately they were so close, ever-present by my side, that I forgot what it was like to not have them.

They were real to me. They sounded just like another voice talking to me. I would turn my head to make sure there was no one next to me, no one shouting at me, but I was always alone. The staff member told me it would take time and patience, and that I would get through this. I hoped so. I needed to heal.

How many years had I tried to heal? So many places without my husband by my side, my family being taken care of by other members of our extended tribe. Jim and Michael were now at Jim's mom's house having dinner. I wished I felt up to caring for them, but I needed to be in a calm setting, simple directions, rest as needed.

For sleep sometimes would come during the day, but the voices would intrude and wake me up. I had tried to lie down but the noise kept me up. I had tried earplugs. That used to help. What else could I do? I distracted myself with sewing, reading, writing, sleeping, art, talking. Nothing seemed helpful. So I wrote some more.

It was quiet at ASSIST. Someone was watching television in the living room, others were sitting in the dining room and the office. Yesterday, there were many people here, with rooms all full. Now, many rooms were empty. I used to interact with the other patients. Now, I smiled and kept to myself.

There were times when I had been hospitalized, that I had tried to help others. I remembered one time when I was in my late twenties and I was locked up, hearing things. I was walking down the hall when I saw a young man sitting alone in his room. I stood in the doorway and smiled at him, asked his name. He had told me and I wished him well.

The next day, there was a poem brought to me. It was from him, about a beautiful angel coming into his room to talk with him. He thought of me an angel! It made me meek, made me put my head down, he was talking about me! I didn't believe that I could be good, sure that I still needed to work on that.

Jim often told me that I was worthwhile. I tried hard to accept his praise and love. I tried hard to be a good woman and mother. I was friendly and nice to most people, but somewhere inside I didn't love myself. Didn't feel like I deserved kindness back. Perhaps that was why I heard the voices. Inner thoughts that felt I deserved to hear berating and destructive thoughts.

My medicine was locked up, so I didn't have access to it. The neighbors tempted me to take them. I wondered what it would be like to swallow all those pills and then go to sleep. Would I wake up to a forgiving God who would take me into His arms and hold me? Would He tell me that it was okay to come home to Him? Or would I end up in darkness, more alone than I felt when I heard the voices? The darkness frightened me , I didn't want to go to a worse space than the one I was in.

Would I be good enough to enter the kingdom of heaven? I was faithful, lived a decent life, prayed and worked and helped others. Was it enough? Would God punish me for taking my own life if I swallowed all those pills or took too much insulin?

But I really wanted to live. I wanted to live. I wanted to live with my family and have my life, a simple life to enjoy. I wanted to work, to play with my family, to go to bingo, to smile and enjoy stolen moments with my husband. I just longed for, wished for, needed, the neighbors to go away.

I didn't feel whole with them in my life. It was always men that screamed at me, taunted me, laughed at me. They stole my peace, they eroded my will to keep on, they scared the shit out of me if I was honest. Imagine minding your own business when suddenly, men were screaming at you and calling you out with hurtful words and it would sound like they were right in the room with you. You would turn around but there would be no one there, no microphone or tape, no other person to verify that you weren't crazy. Your mind was playing with you, and you would have no control over it. It was terrifying. It was cruel. That was daily life for me and I wanted some peace.

They were a symptom. That's what Jim kept telling me. It was a symptom of my illness. Just as if I had to deal with high sugar levels as a symptom of diabetes. It was something to work on, to take medication to cope, and to avoid responding to them.

Symptom's Ache

I awake into the mistake
of the growling men
penned into my mind for far too long.
I belong without the noise,
my boys close by my side.

I've tried so many medications,
stationed at too many therapy offices.

Now I live with the beat of their beliefs
struggling to walk without relief.
Lorazepam calms, palm branches
hung in my home during Lenten prayers,
rare uplifting of my troubles, the woes
erased from such lows.

I'm meant to be free of these harsh
words I have heard forever it seems.
My dreams leave me twisted in the night,
shaping my days with dilemma
as I try to resculpt my thinking,
drinking in the daylight, the sight
of the sun lifting my spirit.

I fear it may one day be too late
when the symptom's ache
wakes the surrender inside
and I'm blind and I find
too much is not enough
to keep me living.

I had tried talking back to them, but then they only got
louder. It was better to push them away, to shake my head
no, to will myself to remain calm and not run screaming
down the street. It gave them less power over me and after
the screams, they would turn down to a murmur. I felt
them still with me though. Like the pinpricks a person gets
on the back of their neck when they feel as if someone is
behind them, but no one is. That's what it was like. Ever

vigilant against their jarring words.

I was working on a children's book and wanted to move the story along. I had talked with Jim last night about different characters that could be introduced along with the main ones. It was nice sharing ideas with my husband, it was comfortable and peaceful. I would go now and spend some time with the other characters. Replace the bad thoughts with creative people that made me feel welcome.

I took a sip of Diet Coke, finished my sentence and turned to work on my other book. This one could really be shared with a wide audience. I enjoyed the desire to create adventures for young people. To place happiness and strength in overcoming obstacles along a child's path, waiting to be discovered. Perhaps that was why I had tried so hard to hold on as a teacher visiting the homes of young children, my job in the islands so long ago. I wanted the small children to have some magic, some fantasy beyond the hardships, and freedom from the abuse that some had. The abuse was what hit me, made me want to scoop up all the children and take them home. I wanted to protect them and I couldn't. Maybe that was why I hid my hearing of the neighbors for so long back then, so I could continue to bring happiness to those little ones who were so sad. But that was what actually magnified the voices of the neighbors back then. The abuse triggered my own sad incidents. Formed the negative talk. It made me hurt so much to see others suffer. It really made me hurt.

CHAPTER TWENTY-SEVEN

I wrote and it felt good to be with the other characters, to get lost in their issues, and thus be able to forget mine for awhile. I stretched and went outside for a cigarette. It was nice outside, cool, crisp. I sat at the picnic table over by the tree with the red bugs. Bugs still spilled out of the dead tree trunk, their red bodies covering the ground. I watched them, wondering what was attracting them to the spot I liked to share with them.

I breathed in. I breathed out. I looked at the sky, blue with wisps of clouds. A nice day to be outside. Soon, Jim would be here to pick me up and take me to church. I felt like that might be helpful. And I was excited to see Jim and Michael.

The car pulled in and I rushed over to greet them. Michael gave me pictures that said he missed me a lot. I thanked him and smiled brightly. We drove to church, parked, and went inside.

The church was quiet, Jesus was in the Tabernacle. We genuflected on our way into His presence. Church began and we sang hymns. Michael sat scrunched up against me as close as he could be. At one point, he sat on my lap and put his head against my neck. He needed me. It felt good to be close to him.

During Mass, Michael and his second grade class went up front before the congregation and placed a heart with their names on it next to a picture of Jesus. It represented them giving their hearts to Jesus. It was very beautiful.

After Mass, we went downstairs and had a potluck with the other second grade families. Michael ate lasagna and pizza, cupcakes and cider. I had casserole, chicken, and crunchy rollers. I took Father aside and he said he would anoint me again. I was glad, it felt so good to be close to Jesus, I wished I always felt this way.

The boys brought me back to ASSIST, and I set to writing my children's book. I was intrigued with the characters, and wanted to help them get to their destination. I felt good, the voices just murmuring in my head.

I took a break and went outside, felt the sun on my face. I closed my eyes and let it warm me. It felt good. It was a nice moment. I breathed in. I breathed out. I was okay.

I let the day be slow, let it drift along with no particular destination. I continued to write. I continued to feel the sun, and thoughts of my family. How much I loved them! Soon I would be home with them, I just had to keep myself safe.

The evening came and I stood outside looking up at the stars with Alex, a staff worker. We talked about the blood moon of last Sunday and how interesting it had been. The stars were bright pinpricks that lit up the night. It was nice to look out and imagine the brightness traveling from so far away to us right here.

The voices crept into my mind, disturbed my vision, and cast my eyes downward. I heard them outside now. I no longer felt clear and calm. I went in and took a Lorazepam, that had been helping calm me. I walked about the living room, had a drink, sat for a few minutes and watched television, anything to distract myself from the noise of the neighbors that felt like it was taking place outside of my head.

Let the Lord Heal

I feel the spirit bursting through
The pain that leaves me numb.
He has come to save my soul,
To replenish my life in whole.
I bend in prayer, I stare aware
That I can live beyond the pain.
The stain of illness presses me
But I can lift and still fly free.
With Jesus ever by my side
I don't have to run and hide.
I've tried my life to work without
The guidance of His ways.
It's been the days filled with prayer
That fill me with His loving care.
My family's faith, my husband's love
Is bound along with mine and God above,
The one true gift divine.
Together we can let the Lord
Heal me in His time.

I got ready for bed, took insulin, crawled into a pair
of Jim's sweatpants that I had so I could feel close to him
when he was not with me. I got into bed, hooked up my
CPAP, and closed my eyes. The voices were loud, shouts
aimed to hurt. I shook my head and thought of my husband. His loving voice was what I wanted to remember. He
loved me, valued me, cherished me. I would get through
this and be home, back to the normalcy of my quiet life. If
only it could be quieter. If only.

CHAPTER TWENTY-EIGHT

In the morning I woke and showered, got ready for the day. Today, I would see Max. Patti was going to take me. I had breakfast, but no Lorazepam. I had run out of it. I tried to distract myself, talked with my husband online, and wrote a little. But my anxiety kept increasing until the voices were shouting down at me from above.

I shook my head. I went to sit with staff. James, the nurse came in and said he had called in some Lorazepam for me and drove to Kinney's to pick it up. It cost a dollar. I took out a dollar to give to him when he got back.

Then, I was placing a Lorazepam under my tongue. I waited for the drowsy feeling to capture me, calm me, relieve the pressure building within my mind, and I wrote.

Anointing with Father Pat

Thank you for the gift, the lift
Of the anointing of my sickness,
the oil on my forehead, on my palms,
the calm prayer of Our Father
with my family close at hand.

I understand that I am a child of God,
my heart is taken up in the present
sight of the help you bring to bless me.

I see the way you care, the prayer
of our faith now upon my soul.
Oh thank you so, I know He hears
My plea, oh please, oh please.

Mia, a staff worker brought me to a morning group. We talked about what goals I had set for the day, how I would know when I was ready to leave ASSIST. I wanted to leave now, but I knew that I wasn't quite safe enough to leave. I still thought about ending my life, still wished for the voices to go away, or for me to just fade into nothingness.

But I was torn. I loved my family and didn't want to hurt them with an act that would be devastating. I knew this deep within me. Knew it from the bottom of my soul, that it would hurt them much more than the voices hurt me. So, I struggled onward.

I wrote. I walked. I smoked. I talked. I made my way through the morning until Patti came to pick me up. She drove me to see Max and we talked about my children's book and the issues in the story. I told her I was feeling a little unsafe. At Max's office, he took me aside to ask me what was okay to talk about in front of Patti. Once that was settled, she came back in and we all talked.

I talked about wanting to diminish the neighbors. Talked about how the medicine made me feel like I was falling out of consciousness, like when I had anesthesia for ECT. It was disconcerting, and traumatic. I thought it might be helping some, but I wasn't sure just how much. We talked about the side effects of high blood pressure and wondered what to do about it.

Mostly, we talked about how I was feeling. I was scared, confused, wanted to run away, but knew there was nowhere to run to, to get away from the voices. I stayed half an hour and then left with Patti.

She drove me back and we talked about fall. Patti talked about the corn maze in Danville that she had been through on the weekend. I listened and thought of autumn moments with my family. Hikes through the woods, apple picking, pumpkin picking and making jack-o-lanterns from them, and trick-or-treating with Michael. Things could be good in the fall too.

Father came and anointed me. He put oil on my forehead and on the palms of my hands. He said a healing prayer and blessing. Michael and Jim were there to share in it. We all prayed the *Our Father* as a group. Jesus loved me. I knew it, I just had to learn to love me too.

It had been a long time, many years, of self-doubt, self-hate, self-destruction in thoughts and words spoken to myself. The voices came to me and hurled the hate, commanded my attention, demanded that I listen. I shook my head no. I would not give in.

For I was a fighter. I had been fighting for over twenty years and much of my life was joyful. I loved my family. I loved my friends. I loved my faith. I needed to love myself. I said I would start with a simple statement.

"I am worthy of life. No matter what I hear, I am valuable. I can choose to live and fight and to keep on."

It was hard work, it was a struggle. But life was made of hardships that sometimes turned into joy. Like having my boys. I loved all three of my children, loved them and protected them, cherished each one of them. I would start to cherish myself, even if it felt strange.

I looked out the window. It was dark out now, the trees dark shapes with silver light in the sky slicing through the branches. The wind swayed them, lulling me outside. I went to close out the darkness and turn towards the light in my room.

For Jesus was my light. He was my salvation. He had died so that I could truly live. I prayed to Him, reached out to Him, clung to His life, His way. I would be strong.

I didn't have a choice. I wanted to fight for my life and I wanted to be in it. I only had one chance at life, time was moving ever forward, there was no turning back the clock.

I sat down in the white wicker chair and stared out into the night sky. The sky had patches of whiteness through the dark trees. I stared up at them, staring at the light that was fading. Soon it was too dark to see any more and I closed the blinds.

I breathed in. I breathed out. I walked about ASSIST. I got a drink of water and it was cold going down. It felt good. I went to the bathroom. I got ready for bed. I put on Jim's sweatpants, my sense of closeness to him. I snuggled down into the blankets of the twin bed. I breathed in. I breathed out. I listened to the neighbors' rantings.

"Kill yourself, you're no good. We're coming to get you." Evil voices that haunted my life. I shook my head and turned towards Jesus.

"Please God, be with me," I said to the room. "Please hold onto me."

I closed my eyes, I put on my CPAP and breathed in and out. In and out. Chanting, "I am valuable. I am worthwhile."

In the morning, I got up and showered, brushed my hair, and went out for a morning cigarette. The sky was blue with white lines of clouds like web strands coating the sky. I lit a cigarette and breathed in and out. I had to stand by the edge of the road now. We were not allowed to smoke on the property. So I stood with my back to the cars that were driving down Pine Street, and looked at the trees bent and gnarled along the creek.

I walked over to the fence that was just across the sidewalk. I looked down at the still water that was at the bottom of a slope. Trees grew right out from the edge of the water forming a canopy around the stream. The water was brown and still. I saw a squirrel climbing one of the trees and I just took notice of its quick movements.

I stood there looking down, imagining the river at Alyssum. How the water's current carried away debris, carried away my worries. I imagined what it would be like to sit by the side of the river on the rocks and just be still. Be still with the peer support workers, patient, waiting for me to begin if I chose. I was still in the silence of the moment, still looking down from the fence. I finished my cigarette and went back into ASSIST.

It was noisy inside ASSIST. Someone was unhappy, calling out. I went and sat in the living room in the rocker. I rocked back and forth, soothing myself. I did a jumble puzzle. I got out my crocheting and moved my fingers with the yarn. It was okay. I was okay.

New people were coming onto the floor and it was noisier. People moving into rooms, people getting settled. I felt like my time here was coming to an end. I was ready to go home and face my fears. I had rested, and now I had more strength to fight off the neighbors.

I was strong. I was capable. I was going to make it. I just wished it wasn't such a hard fight. So many places spent away from my husband. Too many times alone and scared, fighting off the words and hurts of my mind.

Jim and Michael came by for a visit. This was my last night at ASSIST. Michael played on my computer while I talked with Jim. He told me to take things easy when I got home, "Don't rush back into doing everything." I said I would take it easy. It was a good plan. I would go home in the morning. I still had a lot of stories left to write.

I thought back to my younger self. I was older and

wiser now. I was no longer the scared girl, hiding behind the voices. Many people knew I heard voices and they still liked me, some loved me. I could learn to love myself.

I sat and typed out my words. Stretched my mind to remember the strength that I possessed. I was hurting, but I knew I had coping skills. I would remember to use my wise mind, and avoid negative self-talk. I could do this.

I smelled cooking coming from the kitchen and was hungry. Fish frying, maybe some rice. I would go and eat with the other patients, enjoy the conversations, worry less about what was being said in my mind.

But there was laughter, taunting me. I pushed it away. I wrote. I thought about my family. I grounded to the room. I looked at the yellow walls, the blue comforter on the twin bed, the white wicker chair with the green cushion. My computer. I had it under control. I was here, and the voices didn't have power over me. I would remain strong amidst the neighbors.

Still, I wished it was different. Wished I didn't have to hear these voices, these neighbors. They were just noise coming through walls outside of my mind. I could partition them, separate them from my life. I wanted to do that. Needed to do that.

I had applied for substitute teaching and thought that was a good move. I would work part-time at Homegoods, and sub in schools a couple of days a week. It would be good to be with kids again. Older kids I could inspire with books, and writings. I had a lot left to give to people.

I smiled. I pressed an ear plug back into one ear. Sometimes that helped. I listened to the music coming from the kitchen. People were singing to the sounds. People were living normally, doing normalcy. I could too.

I looked out the window and saw David. He lived at a

place called Next Door, another Howard Center program. He talked a lot about confusing things, but he smiled, smoked cigarettes with me, and was kind. He was picking up butts and squatting down to the ground. I watched him bend and stand, bend and stand. He said he was worried about the animals in the area, afraid to get bit. I wished him well. I wondered if he heard voices too.

Yesterday, the Start Team came to see me. They had told me they were recovered peers who helped support people who were trying to heal. They talked about their experiences hearing voices, what medicines they were taking, how long they had been fighting their fights. Some had been fighting as long as I had. We may have even been in the hospital at the same time.

I had been on Smith Three, a locked ward, so many years ago. I had been on Smith Four, an unlocked ward. I had been on Shepherdson Six, the newest locked ward. I had hated every moment locked away. Not enough nature to examine, mostly industrial pipes and vents outside the windows. Not enough sky to see. Not enough color while locked away.

I remembered sitting in a room, doped up, straining to stay awake. No more. I was not as sedated as I used to be. I was on enough medicines that made me sleepy at night, but the feeling went away during the day.

My fear at night grew when I had to take medication. I swallowed the pills but dreaded the feeling that came with them. The feeling of losing control of one's senses, falling back into unconsciousness or sleep. It traumatized me, made me scared. But maybe it was helping with the neighbors so I took them, swallowed the four pills every night in hopes that things would be calmer, quieter.

Well, I was feeling strong tonight. I pushed the neighbors aside, didn't give in to the temptations that they baited me with, yelled to me. Just noise beyond a wall that couldn't hurt me. I stretched and looked back out the window.

It was getting dark out, the sky was still light but the trees were starting to darken in the shadows. Soon it would be black out, and I would spend one more night here at ASSIST. I could do this. I was strong. I was a fighter.

I ate dinner with the other patients and staff. Sat at the table and chatted, smiled even. I made it through the darkening night. I thought about baby steps, small steps to get me to where I was going. I would publish my memoir. My story. My children's books. My poetry again. I was going to reach out and uplift others with my words.

It would be okay to be okay. I leaned back on the twin bed, hoping it was the last one. I closed my eyes and let my breath be the focus. I was okay.

CHAPTER TWENTY-NINE

The year 2016 began with seeming normalcy, a middle-aged couple living together again. Work, kids, small vacations, and the quietness that I savored. The neighbors weren't loud, they were there, but settled behind a wall to my relief.

The ebb and flow of life came back and I let the days carry me. I worked. I lived. I wrote. I played with my family. We took road trips for an hour's drive to Pleasant Valley in Cambridge. Rolled through the hills that moved me, past farmhouses, secluded brooks and bends. It was simply good.

Summer came and with it, the pain of my past caught up with me. I cried, I panicked. My PTSD left me unable to do normal. I beat myself up. I found the guilt so easily wrapped about me like an itchy sweater. I thought I deserved it. I tried hard to push it away. I screamed in therapy, gnashed my teeth, I fought. And the cycle of desperation, all the fear, the delusions that tired my body, tired my mind, did me in. Once again, I was placed at ASSIST.

I couldn't look to the natural for inspiration. I was unable to imagine the perfection of peace penetrating me. I stared out somewhere beyond hope. I was discouraged. Jim visited, held me, cried with me. I was detached, lost.

My psychiatrist at Howard Center talked about a facility in Baltimore that specialized in PTSD. I shrugged. I cried. I decided to take a chance. It was arranged and Jim drove me from the Green Mountains to the big city, the traffic, the noise of a major city.

We stopped at a hotel and made love the night of our

travel. We held onto each other.

We prayed. I said I would fight again. I would learn to cope. He gripped me tightly.

So many nights apart. Too many nights since when we were barely legal and had just wanted to hold each other at night. For years, Jim's job had him away, working twelve-hour shifts at night to support the family. I loved him but wept bitter tears when he was gone.

I learned to accept that it was part of life. Making money, a necessity. And I had always tried to work, always tried to contribute, despite the noise in my head. I rubbed his head and I consoled his loneliness as best as I could. I knew he was hurting, was afraid.

The next morning, we showed up at Sheppard Pratt, an impressive old building. The greens were immaculate, shaved to perfection. A barber couldn't have done better. Flowers were out, whites and pinks. A beautiful August.

Inside, we went through admissions. A nurse took control and searched my bag. Told me I couldn't have my phone, my computer, my lifelines to Jim, to safety. Tears wet my face as I handed them over. The nurse took out a form for me to sign before they would let me enter the wing. It was a form that took away my constitutional right to bear arms in Maryland ever again. It made me sad. It made Jim mad. I had never been violent. We didn't own guns, but always knew that if we wanted to we could, because of the laws first given. I was now excluded from society because I had volunteered to get help with my PTSD. I cried and signed it away.

I said goodbye to Jim. I pressed my body against his, felt his closeness, his love. He tried a smile. I would be brave too. I touched his cheek and then he left.

The nurse took me into a room with another nurse.

This was supposed to be a specialized hospital for PTSD. I wept as they strip-searched me, looked me over, took away my privacy, created a prisoner out of me. I tried to detach, looked out at the roofs of the other buildings, out at the hospital from a small window. No greens, just grays, and brick. And vents, of course. Not at all like Alyssum, or even like ASSIST.

They took me to a room. Surprise, a single bed with a comforter. Bare walls. A high window looking out upon the brick walls of the building. But I could see the sky! I stared at the blue, the wisps of white passing. Thought of lying on a hill as a child, dreams whispered to the sky, the baby blue beginnings of the world.

I attended groups. I followed directions. I began intensive therapy, tried to begin letting out my troubled past. I liked the psychiatrist. The woman doctor prescribed journals, writing as much as possible. I filled a composition book with poetry, pain, and prose.

When the book was filled, I went to the nurse's station and asked for another.

"I'm sorry, only one book per visit." The nurse looked down at me from behind the glass.

"I'm paying $32,000 for one month here. Give me another book."

The nurse shook her head and went back to ignoring me. I shook my head and went to my room. So many stupid rules here. No going outside. I could do that even at the hospital back home. No talking to other patients without supervision. No talking about your pain to one another. We all ignored those last two rules and made up code words to use when staff walked by. Purple was the code for, "stop helping each other with peer support. Talk about the weather."

In my room, I looked at the poems I had put on the walls with tape. The pictures of my family were there too. My sister had sent them. The faces of my boys. The colors of my life.

I took envelopes from get well cards and wrote on them in tiny print. I crafted them carefully with my words because of space.

During the next session with my psychiatrist, I complained that I had no paper. The doctor led me to the nurse's station, demanded a stack of books for me. The nurse on duty sighed and gave them to the psychiatrist. The doctor handed them to me so I could keep on expressing myself, letting out the poisonous thoughts that were consuming me from the past.

I learned to calm my breath, and learned steps to grant forgiveness. I kept talking to other patients. The staff on the floor forbid closeness, and would separate us if they thought we were getting personal. So we kept to our color-coded system. Purple became code for, "quiet the dictators are watching."

As patients, we shared pain at meals, in the living room, and when the staff were walking elsewhere. We were not allowed in each other's rooms, but that was okay. We had a few spaces and times in which we could relinquish our fear and frustration at the system.

They put me on a medication that I was warned, could have side effects. It was going to help with the voices but I had to be careful. I took it, washed it down with water from a dixie cup. But it began to build up in my system. The voices lessened and I felt happier. Peace settled over me and I clung to it with zest. I wrote out my pain, explosions of words blowing relief my way. I shared them with my doctor, with the therapist. I was beginning to make progress.

A month lasted too long, but I got through it and was happier. Jim came and picked me up, eager to have me back. I clung to his body, squeezed him tight. We drove back to our Green Mountains, happy with each other. He was impressed with my behavior. My thoughts and my mind seemed to have been vacated by the neighbors.

My sons were happy to see me. My youngest chatted about the beginning of third grade, his new teacher, his prayers for me. He was joyful. I held his hand as we walked around a furniture store looking for end tables. In the clearance section, we found ones we liked. I felt tired but kept up my spirits. We piled into my husband's Hyundai and loaded the tables. I felt light-headed, tired, so much to shake off. It was a weird feeling.

That weekend, I woke in bed with sweat and hallucinations. I felt sick. Jim checked my temp and it was very high. He loaded me into the car and took me to the ER. The nurse took my temp and rushed me inside to a bed. The doctor on call was a heart specialist. He looked at me and went through several tests. He thought it was meningitis and told me to be still as he took a long needle and inserted it into my spine. Tests were negative. I was very out of it.

The doctor found that the medicine that cured my voices and given me peace, had also given me pericarditis, water around my heart. They stopped the medication and shot me full of antibiotics. I was placed on the cardiology floor of the hospital. They didn't say it, but they were worried.

They gave me an IV, and medications to flush my system. They gave me inhalers so I could breathe better. My lungs hurt too. I slept a lot.

I spent a week there, in and out of sleep. Uncomfortable, tired, and with the onset of voices. I was sad. I had hoped, and prayed they were gone for good but the neighbors were back. They had settled in once more around me.

I slowly healed. They released me from the hospital and told me to use the inhalers to clear my lungs and help me breathe. More medicine to clear up the problem. I spent most days back home in my own bed as my body healed. I had come close to dying. The medicine that had cured me almost killed me.

I had to accept that I must learn to live with the neighbors. There was no magic pill, no flights of fancy to escape from them. I had to cope with my mind. I sat in bed during the day watching the new *Hawaii Five-O*, mindless inaction, my life moving without a mission while I tried to heal. I was still weak. Tired. I tried to accept the terrifying neighbors once more.

Months slid by. I didn't work. I didn't play. I spent most days watching crime shows and physically healing my heart. My husband spent days at work, at home whenever he could be close to me. I loved him. The holidays came and we decorated the house. We bought a tree. Michael listened to Christmas music and smiled. I went out more now and bought gifts when I was able to. I walked about our home. I now sat in the living room. I wrapped presents while Michael was at school.

In January, my depression swelled and I was placed in the hospital in Burlington.

I had to accept the neighbors' loudness that infiltrated my thoughts. I was so sad.

I still wrote poetry. I gave poems to other patients who were so sad and lost there on the floor. I wrote about seeing them. Being with them. I wrote about my wishes to be in nature as I was confined to the muted halls of the hospital.

Three months of turmoil, three months of pain, released again. Radical Acceptance, an important piece; I agreed to go through the Crossroads' program, a day-program to help me cope with life.

I left the hospital and began to meet in a circle of plastic chairs, a leader prescribing new ways to think. Release of stress, mindfulness, dialectical behavior therapy (DBT). With it, I learned to stay in the moment, to push past fears. Slowly life came back, and I accepted that the neighbors were part of that.

Life rushed at me as the summer exploded into beauty in Vermont. I took day trips to observe the landscape. We went to the lake to soak up liquid relief from anxiety. We rolled through the mountains of Stowe. We learned to live each day.

Michael started fourth grade. He was excited, happy to have his mom better. I drove him to school in the mornings, picked him up at the end of each day. We sang to CD's of Christmas music that he loved. I laughed at his boisterous ways. And, I loved it all.

Fall came and I thought back to my childhood hill, the space that now seemed bigger than before. A message about the simplicity of youth. Natural surroundings, a way to live between the scents of freshness, flowers, and sunshine.

I wrote more. I loved more. I went to a new therapist who I began to open up with about my trauma. I had never spoken of the details of my pain, the terrors it brought, the flashbacks. I let it all out. I was brave. I believed in the help I was getting from this lady.

Fall moved to winter and whiteness spread over the

land. A clean covering, a new possibility to uncover with my son. We pressed the snow, we molded it, we used our bright red shovels to clear the drive. And we laughed.

Christmas came with all my boys at home. My two oldest trying to pay off loans and save for places of their own. I secretly loved having them all back, knowing they were safe. I prepared meals for them all. I cleaned. I loved.

January came again and with it, my sadness that seemed to settle down on me at this time each year. They placed me back in the hospital. I wasn't as down as last year, but still needed extra help. The doctors tried to offer ECT. I was stressed about it, weighed the option with my therapist who actually visited me in the hospital, and who also agreed with me that it was more traumatic than helpful.

I met with patients and gave them my words as gifts. One of the workers who supervised me until I could be safe alone was very social. I learned he was a jazz musician and he told me about his cousin in Kool and the Gang. He had a rich dark face and white, white teeth. His stories made me smile. I liked him. The next night, when he came in, I had a poem for him. I read it to him, showing that I saw him, and he cried. I gave it to him and he took it while wiping his eyes. He thanked me for capturing him, his life, his moments. I smiled. I helped.

I decided I was best when I helped others. I wrote more, thought less of the haunting words that spun within me. I agreed to fight on. I worked hard and was able to go back to my family once more.

I felt such guilt sometimes. My illness created chaos when I wasn't around to help my family. But without me ever in their lives, they said they would be worse. They needed me and I needed them.

I learned to forgive. I crafted. I worked on my physical

health. I loved my family, loved my husband. I went to a writers' group and shared my work. Shared some of the rawness that was found in my poetry.

Perhaps I could accept that I was human. That for some reason, most likely genetics, coupled with repeated trauma, I had been marked in harmful ways. But I knew I also possessed light, there was still goodness inside me. I knew I had to believe in that as my purpose, a foundation for my life.

I blogged about my pain. I started a poetry movement on Facebook by writing poems for people, to uplift them, to find the goodness in the world and share it. People responded. And I smiled.

Summer came as Michael finished fourth grade. He cried in my arms in the car as we picked him up. He loved his teacher so much he wasn't ready to give her up and go to the next grade. I held him tight, kissed his cheek as he held onto me, his mother.

I shared music with my son. We listened to hymns, we listened to funk, we listened to rock and pop. He tried learning to dance like Michael Jackson. We listened to *Don't Take the Girl* and my son said it hit him right in the heart like their recent trip to Arlington Cemetery. At the cemetery, he had said, "Mom this place could really change a person."

I loved his sensitive nature. I had to protect him still, he was so gentle, so kind. I embraced the days with him and my husband. I made meals for all the boys at night. I cleaned, and I laughed more. I shared my writings.

And I was happy. Everything was better with the green of Vermont. The flowers planted, the perennials coming back into bloom. And I danced in my mind as I swayed in life. My ankle hurt. I sprained it in March and it wasn't healing. Next week there would be an MRI to determine if the ligaments were cut.

Today, I was going to play bingo with a friend. Last weekend I had stood at a wedding reception, my sixth one, and read my poetry about the love and happiness that the newly joined couple shared. People responded. I made others happy. I had a purpose.

My husband held me at night. I loved the last few years, him working days, working so hard for us. I wished my writing could support him, take away his stress and hardship, give him a rest. I entered my first poetry contest and won first place.

Perhaps I could write out my story. Share it with the world. Perhaps help a young girl getting mixed up by the madness of teenage years. Perhaps I could distill wisdom from my own troubled ways.

Nature was key. I closed my eyes and thought of sitting on the beach before the ocean. The too-short days by the sea. The smell of salt, the inspiration for a poem, the point of life waved in by the crests crashing on the beach.

Perhaps it was a moment crushed between two Green Mountains in a valley. My stay at Alyssum set me on the path to healing. Struggling with the despair, willing it to culminate, to disperse it from my body. To let it out like others who had gone through similar pain. I opened my eyes and thought back to the beginnings of my healing there at the retreat house.

There, I had discovered that I could use my gift of writing to really heal. To dispel the depression, the neighbors, the voices, the anger and humiliation that penetrated my world.

I had a gift. A gift from God. It was from His life that I had been given the words that formed from my fingertips out and onto the pages or my screen. I thanked God for the gift of language. I prayed someone could be helped by my experiences. Perhaps there was someone out there just waiting to hear what I had to say. And it could help them be strong too.

I thought of my time at the retreat house, the farmhouse and beyond to the river. The river had been of great beauty, to sit beside it and throw away painful memories with each rock flung into the water. I wondered if I was stronger now than I had ever been.

I thought of the river. That's where I had found hope. Was it the river that wound through the narrow valley or was it my writing of the river that unwound the pain in my heart? I wondered if it could be both. I knew that someday I would go back to Alyssum, visit the farmhouse. There was a new addition off the kitchen, but the view would be the same.

It would remain a small house in a valley within the Green Mountains of Vermont. Farmer's fields with cornstalks laden with the corn just ripening. There would be the smells of rural living. The manure from the cows in the barn rising to meet the scent of cut grass and garden's growth. There would be vegetables and flowers in the greenhouse to bring to the dining table. Fresh-cut scent of purples, greens, yellows, and white flowers. Handpicked red tomatoes, sliced and salted, a taste of home.

And the sun would shine down just above the trees atop the mountains, sundown by the river, edged in shadows. The river that never slept, kept up its movement, its rhythmic dance over boulders and stones that dotted its body. I thought of standing right there by the river, watching it go, letting go of struggles, letting them go elsewhere with the water as the sun slid down beyond the pines.

The night animals would come stand by the riverside. Deer, fox, maybe a coyote, drinking the water that
sliced through the field. Mountains sheltered bears as well.
There had been a time when I was there that I went to
the river in the fading light and sat on the bank observing
the surroundings. I listened to the river gurgle, listened to
the buzzing insects coming out. I sat there and stayed in
the moment. When I decided it was time to go back to
the house, I looked across the river to the other side. Eyes
peered back at me, three sets. I stood up fast then, wondering what was there just beyond the edge of the river in
the tree line. Bears? I didn't know, but I was curious. What
were they? Would they come down to the river with me
there?

I kept staring at those eyes lit up from within the
shadows of the trees. I wondered if it was a mother and
two cubs. They didn't move, just stayed in one place, staring back at me. After a time, I turned away and headed
back up the small hill to the farmer's field. I walked across
his field still littered with clay shells from his son's rifle. I
walked past the cows in the barn, over the mounds of manure and dirt. Darkness was approaching with just a few
lines of light remaining to guide me back.

I had reached the grass and walked past the greenhouse. Shoots were coming up because of Karen's green
thumb. I walked up the small hill past the fire pit, and on
up to the white gravel drive.

I slapped my feet against the drive, against the land.
I was here. I was alive and things in my head were quieter for now. I remembered that walk, that inspiration that
things could be better. I stood by the door to the farmhouse
looking out at the last moments of daylight that lingered
over the valley. It was getting harder to see beyond the

silhouettes of the fields, those rolling hills that bordered to the tree line and the river. Such evergreen trees that filled the land with their straight trunks and dark green needles, the rich scent of pine sap.

Spring had arrived but the chill of winter could still be felt felt in the air. I shivered as I looked out into the darkening fields. I wondered if the mother bear and her cubs were now back at the river. Life depended on the water, grew in its currents. And the river kept up its movement through light and darkness, kept to its rhythmic dance through the valley. I thought I was ready to go back to the rhythm of my old life, wind through the days with my own family.

The Road Home

I am not alone for I am blessed with a man that holds my hand,
walks by my side, lifts my chin up to his when I am torn inside.
Brushed with the fear of my disease, frightened by the noise of my
mind, he kisses away my fear. He is brave, courage keeps him at
work when all he wants is to unwind with a drink, a smile, a mixed
cocktail of inspiration from our creative, sensual senses. Oh how I
adore him, how I long to drive down the interstate, our hands
enclosed, loud rock and voices shrilling out the beats, the notes, the
words to the eighties when we met.
Seventeen in the sun, smiles and sadness still but oh

the ride we have
been on! I close my eyes this morning, feel the weight
of his worry
turn to prayer, dare to believe in our dreams at almost
fifty...
much time perhaps left to explore the back roads of
our destiny. I
travel to him, meet him in his sleep, kiss his face, hold
our love close,
cradled in each other's arms.

I thought back to the time spent in so many places. Too many places, not enough peace. I wanted someone to take away the pain of hearing the neighbors. I was looking for someone to ease the troubles that I faced. The neighbors' voices echoed from my past. Painful thoughts that I felt at one time, remained in some way. I wished I could develop the peace that I had felt sometimes there by the river, where I had come to terms with a lot of my past. I just wished I could be rid of the symptoms I still struggled with.

Me, a middle-aged woman, imagined myself pressed against my husband. I would be curled into his arms, resting my head on his shoulder. I decided it was good to fight for this. Doctors could play with the medicine, but I needed to do the work. I could do it with help.

I had been in therapy for most of my life, ever since I was a girl of thirteen. Now, for the first time, I was being treated by a woman to whom I opened up, and for the first time, shared my true history. The first time I was able to speak the words of pain out loud.

My therapist was a lesbian with Jewish alphabet symbols tattooed up and down her arm. She listened like Jim. She encouraged me, unlike the first psychiatrist I had seen at thirteen. In that first encounter with psychiatry, I was crammed between my parents, with the three of us sitting across from an old doctor asking me what my problems were. As if it were really that simple.

I thought back to Mindy, the therapist that had been motherly. She had helped me get through hearing the neighbors during the first year they began to visit me. I remembered the terror that their words instilled in me, calling Mindy one afternoon from downtown in the mall when the neighbors became especially loud. Mindy had talked to me, soothed my pain, and kept me in the present.

So many years being disabled by depression, PTSD, bipolar, with days dominated by the neighbors. Time had passed but I could still become defeated by the threats and fatigue of my disease. My husband had always been with me, holding me, walking side-by-side as we both fought. I was a fighter, and knew that deep inside. I wanted to overcome the blackness that enveloped me, that dark hole that held me back from living. I decided I would continue to live as if the neighbors were just voices that I heard through the wall, from another life, not mine.

"We're coming to get you. You need to die."

I would be the light that shone into the darkness. I would light up the world with hope for a better way of living. I would be like those eyes staring back at me from across the river, a light from within the dark, despairing landscape of my mind. There was strength in living. I would fight. I closed my eyes and drifted off to the now, the quiet surrounding me, letting peaceful solitude overcome me. I breathed in and out, closed my eyes and nestled against my own pillow. I was home with my love beside me. And it was good. So good as I fell to sleep with the noise of the neighbors stirring behind a wall.

CHAPTER THIRTY

Resting between Recoveries

I rest in pieces of survival
Through the months, the years, the moments that I
have escaped
the madness I met in my youth.
There are parts that I find solace, comfort, joy with
my family.
My boys and husband gift me tranquil days that de-
termine me to keep on.
There are also parts that fit me into nature
and I become as calm as a palm tree in the sun,
gently swaying, leaves turning, strong roots holding.
Pieces of my writing temper and also revive
Some of the betrayal of my mind.
I dwell deeply in stories I create.
I separate myself from the pain, the stagnant days of
unrest.
I set off without a written end, the blank page filling
with quests
That settle my insides,
leave me relaxing from tightly held shoulder muscles.
There are parts that can't be fixed.
Broken sentiments that I find no glue or clue for cure.
In the cycles of extremes, I am taken out of the days
routine
And brought away for rest.
It is hard to determine, to agree that I need the rest.
For really I usually know I need the muted walls,
the soothing voices, the quiet to control

The loudness that rings inside.
Forty times I have been shut off in a meditative cell,
asked to control
The burnt ember of my youth that was staked, lit,
and enflamed in the anger of men.

I am the one that must keep myself still.
To breathe in and out and settle the exotic thought of
anger.
To no longer burn but cool my thoughts. Keep
breathing.

Perhaps when I find myself too sad I will close my
eyes and go, but not to Innisfree,
no that's another poet's romance.
I will settle my sagging shoulders into the farmhouse
residence in Rochester.
I will walk the farmer's fields littered with the
remains of his sons still practicing their shooting.
I will stride past the barn that is half-built into the
meadow's hill. The cows will not have visible breaths
like before, they will be swishing their tails at the heat
that brings the flies, while I stomp my presence into
the field.
I will wade through the tall weeds and flowers strewn
about the edge of the river that flows on. I will mold
my toes over the worn rocks on the bank and sink
them into the water.
Perhaps I will toss my despair into the movement,
watch it head downstream, never to return.

Or I could accompany the other patients from
the white rooms, the silent windows, the held in

breaths... out to the walled-in courtyard.
Back where the young nurses, not yet having to dye
their hair, converse. They speak of new tattoos and
free days.
I will settle on a granite bench and observe the words,
the moments, the tempo of this day for I am a writer
even without a pen.
The cherry tomatoes that line the walls will be plump
and red. Red like one of the nurse's lipstick. Does she
hope to impress another doctor?
I will watch the slow rhythm that forms the crew of
sadness. Watch some walk in their steps, some reach
out to touch the roughness of the wall, some twirling
a finger on a blade of grass.

The color of the courtyard is a crisp yellow day of
summer
With a blue field above the depression.

I will lift off my bench and feel lighter.
If a bird I would fly to a tree. To the highest branch
And look down on all that is alive. All that is
survivable.
I would shake my wings out and stretch them ever so
wide.
I would lift into the blueness so much like my eyes.
I would circle the world, watch the cycles churn like
that river.
Watch the emotions drain from my veins.
I would fill myself on berries and beliefs that I am
beautiful.

I would meet myself back at seventeen

When the anger consumed.
I would hold her when she was first locked away.
I would listen and not hide her from happening.
I would let her claim her courage,
Turn down the recommendation
To reflect and to rest away from college
In a muted room of the hospital.
I would visit her there if she went still.
I would watch her with other teens cast off.
Hidden
From society, I would shake myself
And do what I wanted
Not wait locked up until reasonably preferred.

Oh, and I would visit the night
before my eighteenth birthday in December.
When I escaped to the outside winter.
Where
Three of us made our way through the windings of
the old hospital.
To the mighty oak door.
We opened the magnificent stained door to the hill
outside.
Snow was just falling.
We smiled without thought.
Our feet, bare, pressed into the carpet of whiteness on
the ground.
A layer of flakes floated about,
We caught the snow like glitter and twirled in the
moonlight.
We didn't run. We didn't hide. We danced
To the music of memories.
We were youth without worry

On a hill with the snow crystals containing
All we needed.

Yes, I still need to rest. Still need to pause
And reset the possibility that I still have things left to
do.
I imagine more, I dream in days and nights
And often more when I am awake.

I often revisit the times before my trauma,
Before the strands of normalcy got pulled apart.
I sew the images together into poems.
I listen to the elements from the past,
The stirrings that pull at my heart,
That beat out in couplets, and rhyme
And free verse.
I hold onto the patterns that bring peace.
And I breathe it in.
I escape the frenzy and despair
By holding onto the family I continue to raise.
I partner with my husband even if it is just to trim the
hedges
Out front, take in the breath of cedar
While we are together.
I planted a tree this summer, three inches high,
Enclosed in a milk container for protection.
Perhaps Perhaps Perhaps
Someday the crab apples will blossom,
Bloom, ripen for the birds.
And then perhaps I will watch the birds reap
The harvest I have given out over the years.
I will watch them soar into the heavenly blueness
above,

Stretch out their wings and glide in rest.
Peaceful rest.
And the happiness that flutters inside will come to
settle
Permanently in my mind
And someday rest will resolve the battles I still wage.

Almost Fifty

I am not alone for I am blessed
with a man that holds my hand,
walks by my side, lifts my chin up to his when I am
torn
inside. Brushed with the fear of my disease,
frightened by the noise of my mind,
he kisses away my fear. He is brave,
courage keeps him at work when all he wants is to
unwind with a drink,
a smile, a mixed cocktail of inspiration
from our creative, sensual senses.

Oh how I adore him,
how I long to drive down the interstate,
our hands enclosed, loud rock and voices shrilling
out the beats, the notes, the words to the eighties
when we met.
Seventeen in the sun, smiles and sadness still, but oh
the ride we have been on!

I close my eyes this morning, feel the
weight of his worry turn to prayer,
dare to believe in our
dreams unfolding now at almost fifty...

Natural Order

I clip the bush out front,
snip branches too long, the ones
that don't conform to the shape,
the style, the moment I'm trying to make of the front
yard.
The blades zip together, sharp in their cuts as I continue to
pare the leaves, the withered, the dead.

For my life could be the springtime of this plant,
the flowering bud, the rich green of each leaf, the
dark soil
feeding, the water quenching.
And I could be okay to be okay.
I don't have to hurt over the years that the bush
didn't grow, didn't make a statement for the yard.

I cut and prune, careful in my design.
in with the breath, I cast off the unwanted like the
trauma, littering the ground with it,
molding my perfection. I stand back to admire
and realize there will always be more
To take away, but perhaps

I can let it go back to the wild living,
creating its own way to be happy in the wonder of
itself.
I close my scissors. Let them rust.
Let the beauty be in its living.

I sit with sunglasses on

protecting my view,
as I watch the natural order
take care of my yard.
And it's okay.

ABOUT THE AUTHOR

A native of Vermont, **Jodi Girouard** has been writing stories since she could hold a pencil. She is a wife, a mother, a poet, and a survivor of mental illness. She has previously published two collections of her poetry: *Body Language; a woman's voice* and *Faces in the Crowd*. Her recent essay, "Within the Fields of Possibilities" is included in the 2019 edition of *Much Madness*. She has won several writing contests and her poetry is featured in the July 2019 edition of *Wordgathering*.

Jodi has lived with mental illness for most of her life and is active in promoting conversations that aim to reduce the stigma associated with such illness. She is a motivational speaker helping to raise awareness through openness about the symptoms many people face. In addition, Jodi speaks about her spiritual life which also helps heal.

She says, "Recovery is a daily action, fighting severe mental illness with a team approach, medication, and therapy." She writes about it in much of her poetry which she shares on her website at JodiGirouard.com.

ACKNOWLEDGMENTS

This book could not have been written without my husband, Jim Girouard. Without his support, advocacy, and love I wouldn't be alive to share my story. Finding him at seventeen, falling in love together, and then living through the ebb and flow of my illness has brought us closer and strengthened our bond. I am forever grateful for this man who, during college, found out I was pregnant with our first child, and took the first job he could find that had health insurance. He toiled for many years working his way up from running a hamburger machine in a meat plant to running the plant in his early twenties. He is hard working, loyal, and my very best friend.

My sons are the compassion, the care, the joy of my life. Three very different boys with the same joy and love that I bestow on each one. They bring me from the sadness back to the safety of living and loving.

So many therapists, psychiatrists over the years, and the staff at Howard Center. Mindy Evnin, Oliver Quayle, Max Miller, Sue Shaffer, Patti Bauerle, Marlene Williamson, Maureen Joyce, Megan Dunston, Dr.Lasek, Dr Chen, Dr. Jacobson, Dr. Naylor, and countless support workers.

For Stephen Kastner who promoted, published, and helped bring my creativity to life, who I am privileged to call my friend. For Sarah Procopio, Michelle Walker Place, Robin Lawson, Toni Menard Zeno, Maribeth Nichols, and Tina Menard who supported my story by helping with the Book Trailer. For my sister, Tammy, who continued to support me when I was away by helping with my children and visiting me. For my mother, Marlene, who loved me no matter how much I struggled, and continues to love and support my children. For Sue and Jim for always being there to feed my family when I was away, and for always holding me as their own child.

And for the ones I lived with while away in the agony, the struggles, the pain, and sometimes finding joy in our companionship locked away with only hope and a friendly face, in a patient, to see. For all the ones that I have uplifted with a poem, for the ones that uplifted me, for the ones I have yet to meet and see beyond the stigma to the person before me.

And I am grateful, so grateful, for the environment of Vermont. For the colors I crave in the woods, the flowers blooming magnificent scents, the hills to discover, the fields to run through, and the exquisite wonder of my early childhood gifted to me by my parents.

Finally, I am also grateful for the Mount Philo Road Crew. The friends that journeyed with me up our hill back in childhood to where we found life lived freely in each moment. Where kids didn't isolate, didn't have to hide inside but could find fascination with one another alive in the green of Vermont. And for the ones reading this who need to know, if you were beside me right now, I would hold your hand, I would truly see the one you needn't hide anymore.

ORGANIZATIONS

These are the places that have helped me over the past thirty plus years when I dearly needed them. All but Sheppard Pratt Hospital (Maryland) are located in Vermont:

Alyssum
ASSIST
Brattleboro Retreat
Crossroads
Howard Center
Mercy Connections
Northwestern Counseling
Respite House
Seneca Center
Sheppard Pratt Hospital
University of Vermont Medical Center
Visions and the Day Program
Westview House

.